Happÿ bank

The bank that changed the world

Dear Bronwen,

Vishal Gupta
Cyrus Gonda

What an AMAZING
SMILE & energy U have.
Love U always. Keep
Smiling

28/2/20

EBD
EMBASSY BOOKS
www.embassybooks.in

Happyness Bank
© Vishal Gupta

This edition first published in 2019

Published in India by:
Embassy Book Distributors
120, Great Western Building,
Maharashtra Chamber of Commerce Lane,
Fort, Mumbai - 400 023.
Tel : (91-22) 22819546 / 22818567.
Email : info@embassybooks.in
Website : www.embassybooks.in

Distribution Centres:
Mumbai, Bangalore, Kolkata, Chennai,
Hyderabad, New Delhi, Pune

ISBN: 978-93-88247-33-7

Printed & Bound in India by Quarterfold Printabilities, Navi Mumbai

Testimonials

Suhas Warke
(DIG, Anti Terrorism Squad)

The idea given in this book, if successfully implemented, would be the most potent and effective idea to fight hatred and communal disharmony. I believe that if the message in this book is imbibed by society, we should soon have a more peaceful world.

Dr. O. P. Kapoor

I have seen Vishal grow up in front of my eyes, and have seen him progress both personally and professionally, very closely. He exudes brilliance in everything he does, and is always brimming with new ideas.

Vishal's ideas grew bigger and bolder as he grew older, proof of which you hold in your hand today in the form of this book – The Happyness Bank. Having a rare ability to implement his visualized thoughts into physical reality, I have no doubt that Vishal will change the world for good with his noble ideas. In today's day and age where people only think about themselves, vishal is one of the few people who is taking a courageous step to change the face of humanity.

Happyness Bank, I believe is the best prescription for a happy and healthy society that we all aim to live in. I wish Vishal all the best.

Adv Mrunalini Deshmukh

I had the fortune to go through the book authored by Mr. Vishal Gupta and the same is happily called the Happyness Bank.

I found the book very interesting informative and refreshing.

As a lawyer dealing with emotionally high strung cases, it does create, a lot of stress and at times negativity. Despite the same, the mark of a true lawyer is to deal with each case with positivity, optimism and in a constructive manner.

Vishal with his humility, and his ability to see and integrate all aspects of life, has also always been someone who chooses to focus on a solution, rather than on a problem. I am sure this book, The Happyness Bank, which is an extension of Vishal's personality, is going to help the challenging situations the world faces today.

I am extremely delighted to see the that Vishal, in his inimitable style of thinking, has come up with such a unique, interesting, yet simple solution to change the world.

I highly recommend this book to EVERYONE, and congratulate Vishal for gifting humanity such a wonderful idea.

Aasha Warriar
(C.R.T., Director, Clover Leaf Learning Academy Pvt. Ltd. Trainer –TASSO Institute Netherland)

An overview and a new, much needed vision of the world, if each one can make it happen. With the global energy shift we are witnessing since the last 20 years and which will continue for alteast another 20 years, this book couldn't have come at a better time.

Urvashi Saxena
(Ex-Chief Commissioner of Income Tax, Mumbai)

It is my proud privilege and honour to write a testimonial for this wonderful book.

Having read the book written so lovingly by the young author duo Vishal Gupta and Cyrus Gonda I have to admit, at the outset, that I was not prepared to see what I got. At first I thought it would be yet another self-help book written by some indulgent and enterprising young professionals but after going through the contents I have to change my opinion.

It is a book whose time has come. Not only is it topical and contemporary but also written with a lot of conviction and sensitivity; truly, a labour of love. It is written in a simple but beautiful language and engages the reader at a very esoteric level. The pursuit of happiness is a universal phenomenon and has been craved by mankind from times immemorial. As we struggle to achieve true happiness, the challenge before us is to find a balance between our personal goals and to align them with the larger goals at the national and inter-national levels. I find the unique concept of the bank of good deeds and good karma enunciated in this book will go a long way in fulfilling that need. I am sure that the passbook of good deeds will dispel the pall of gloom and cynicism which is engulfing our country and eventually raise India's ranking on the world's happiness index.

The book is beautifully illustrated and embellished with appropriate and inspirational quotes from great men. I do hope and wish that the practical suggestions given at the end would serve as great enables from the public at large and that the government and corporate leaders would take full advantage of these doable guidelines. I am confident that the issues addressed in this book will lead to ethical solutions peppered with empathy and enlightenment which would result in true happiness. I shall also end with a quotation "Transformation of humanity might be our only hope for survival." Stanislov Graf.

Zakkaullah Siddiqui
(CMD Zaka Group of Travel & Cargo CompaniesGSA - Saudi Arabian Airlines)

Dear Vishal

Indeed was delighted and feel privileged having received copy of "Happyness Bank" dedicated especially to your Mom. It goes without saying that it includes your dear Father Mr. Vinod Gupta.

While having a glance I find many of the valuable quotes from Buddha to Prophet Mohammed.

It will go a long way to achieve happiness in life, and people can open their account today itself with no paperwork and cost and can enjoy the benefits and dividends without any investment.

Your vision is highly appreciated and very practical in this materialistic world. **May God Bless You !**

I pray for your continued endeavours towards happiness of the unemployed, frustrated lot and the growing population in leaps and bounds.

Yaashree Himatsingka
(Head Girl - Cathedral and John Connon School)

I really like how the concept (of managing a personal log of good deeds, similar to a bank account) is conveyed through a story. This makes it clear, engaging and easy to follow.

The illustrations are delightfully detailed and suit the style of writing - descriptive and emotive. The cover is simple and clean; The smiley face on the 'y' is tactfully placed and contributes some liveliness.

The main idea (if you do good, good will be done to you) is very relatable as it springs directly from the spiritual principle of *karma* (that an Indian audience is sure to be familiar with).

While I didn't fully agree with the idea of receiving "rewards" in exchange for doing good deeds, I do feel that it will be very effective in encouraging others to do good. In that sense, it certainly fulfills its purpose.

Anil Harish

I have known Vishal since a number of years as he attended my lectures at Government Law College. He is a multifaceted person bubbling with energy and new ideas.

One of his new ides is what I hold in my hand as I write this.

We are at a time in evolution when man seems to have obtained all kinds of materialistic comforts but does not have the most important thing- Happiness.

Happiness seems to have eluded even the most rich, famous and beautiful. Millions of people are suffering from depression, fatal diseases, crime and terrorism. Everyone wants a more peaceful, beautiful life but nobody knows "HOW?"

To answer "HOW"? we need thought leaders with new refreshing ideas.

Vishal is one such thought leader, who through his book, which is aptly titled 'The Happiness Bank' has introduced to the world a new, simple but revolutionary idea.

I hope this book will inspire people to relook at their lives and bring about positive everlasting change.

I wish Vishal all the best!!

Happyness Bank

Contents

Dedication

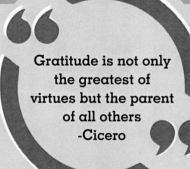

Gratitude is not only the greatest of virtues but the parent of all others
-Cicero

It is said that God created a Mother since HE could not be there to help everyone at the same time. Like the rays of the sun empower our very being on this planet, true to her name, my mother Kiran Gupta empowered me with her love, support and wisdom.

This book is dedicated to you and all that you have done for me, Maa. You are the best!

Vishal Gupta

I would like to dedicate this book to all true animal lovers, who have in their own way saved and eased the lives of these innocent creatures.

Cyrus Gonda

Acknowledgment

Happÿness Bank

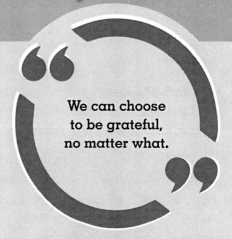

> **We can choose to be grateful, no matter what.**

I t's a blessing to receive a wonderful opportunity like this, to give gratitude to people who have influenced and impacted my life, profoundly. These people have been instrumental in motivating me to not only to write this book, but also polish my thoughts on life in general.

I thank my father, Vinod Gupta, for being my constant pillar of strength, and always being there to support me in his own special way. I thank the two most important women in my life, Bhawana and Jiya, for their continuous support while writing this book, and also through the course of my life. They have been both, my well-wishers and critics, which has tremendously helped me in various ways.

My utmost gratitude to Phiroza, who played the role of a guiding angel in the early stages of my life, and nudged me to perceive life in a more constructive way. I also thank Kulwant Singh for being a role model, and making me believe that it is possible for human beings to be happy in all circumstances.

Aknowledgement

I thank my dear friend Gauraj Shah, for all the support he has given me over the years. I further thank him for agreeing to lend us his wonderful name in the story of Happyness Bank. I would also like to thank Indira Debbie, Anoop Pandey, Satyajit Fovkar, Shivani Agarwal, Parvati Gupta, Neha Chhajalane and Amit Bhatia, for taking out time to have countless hours of extremely mind stimulating discussions on happiness and its pursuit. My gratitude to Dilip Ahuja, and Deepa Shah for helping me bring out my creativity.

Rahul Gaikwad has done a brilliant job with the sketches in the book, and I thank him wholeheartedly for them. This book would not have looked so beautiful without the creativity and layout skills of Paru Shethna.

Ishita came on board to edit and proof read the book, but ended up making the book her own. She has done a fantastic job in not only aiding to give the book a structure, but has also added her spiritual and psychological insights. I thank you from the bottom of my heart, for the love and support you have bestowed during the process of making this book, and also truly believing in the concept of The Happyness Bank.

Without the guidance of my wonderful friend of many years, Sohin Lakhani, this book would not have manifested in physical reality. I am grateful to him for guiding me to books and people that have enabled me to put my thoughts on paper, giving the idea of this book a beautiful form- one that I hold very dear to my heart.

I conclude by thanking all those I haven't mentioned, for playing a role in my life in a small or big way, that has helped me to learn, grow, and evolve into a better human being.

- **Vishal Gupta**

Introduction

Happÿness Bank

> Let your good deeds be like rain. Drop a little everywhere.

The world we live in today, is dismal and bleak. With each passing day, this planet which we call our dear Mother Earth, is only becoming a more violent place to inhabit. Mankind appears to be rapidly hurtling towards self-destruction, becoming its own worst enemy. Each century is getting bloodier than the previous one. Well over a hundred million people lost their lives in the most grotesque way, in the two world wars. Furthermore, if the various terrorist attacks and violent crimes are included, the death tolls are mind boggling.

Man has made exponential progress in reaching outer space - even journeyed to Mars, yet, he has failed to conquer his own inner space. Nuclear power was created to harness energy and help human kin, but it is currently being misused to develop the potential to destroy billions. As man improves in technology, he also improves his efficiency in techniques of destruction. A huge percentage of people around the world go off to bed without having a single square meal throughout the day. Unemployment is on the rise, and so is the global population, all fighting for life's basic necessities.

Do we not see, every single day, that killing one terrorist gives birth to ten more? All of us live in perpetual darkness of anxiety, swinging from one fear to another, without even consciously realizing it. We focus more on planning for future debacles and on what could go wrong, instead of infinite opportunities for things to go right. We cover our way of thinking with blankets of hopelessness, jumping from one high to another, and curb the void within us.

Is there a solution and way out of this mess? If there is, what and where is it? Is an eye for an eye or a bullet for a bullet going to solve any of our current problems? How do we put a halt to all the lunacy around us? How do we get out of the ugly mayhem that we have around ourselves? As much as we put our trust in external sources like the Government and certain organisations, the truth is, they don't really have a concrete answer. Their strategies could be brilliant, but they are pretty short lived. No one seems to have any long term ideas or visions on changing the current scenario. Whether we admit it or not, despite our different socio-economic and cultural backgrounds, all of us have the same questions playing like a broken record in our tiny minds.

We are all looking for a way out. We are all treading on a path that would lead us somewhere, and help us in becoming **HAPPIER** individuals. Happiness in today's age is chased like an elusive animal, without us making an effort to realize, that the solution lies in changing ourselves, our perceptions, and our rigid beliefs. Most of us resist change in any form, both consciously and sub-consciously, choosing to rot with the same frame of mind, for years together. We forget that the very core of human existence is **CHANGE.** It is a clichéd phrase, but it is absolutely true- *Change is the only constant in the Universe*. Without a paradigm shift in human consciousness, there is never going to be a solution. The shift has to begin with us. With a simple yet powerful step of consciously choosing and making a committed effort to work on ourselves, in order to change our lives, our destiny, and eventually, the destiny of man-kind.

With the grace of God, I had everything that one would ever want to lead a happy and content life. The finest education, a beautiful wife and daughter, a great job as a well-established and accomplished criminal lawyer, a house and a car. Yet, there was always a part of me that felt a deep void within. The same questions that plague humanity today, bogged me down as well. Those questions made me look for answers at different times, in different places, with different people.

As it has been said by some of the greatest sages and masters, happiness is not a destination, but a journey; I started treading the not-so rosy path in the search of ideas and answers, and find something that truly made me happy. This enabled me to study almost all the religious texts such as the Bhagvad Gita, Quran and Bible; the works and lives of enlightened masters such as the Buddha, Ramana Maharishi, Swami Vivekananda, Lao Tzu, Paramhansa Yogananda, Isan, Tilopa, Narpa, Malerepa, and the likes. I noticed a common thread in all of them. They all spoke of the same thing in different ways, in different languages, and with different explanations- *when you do something good, it comes back to you, in manifolds.* I also realized, whatever we lose, always returns in another form. Just as the tree loses its leaves every winter, new growth cannot come without loss.

It was after these realizations that I started experiencing inexplicable joy while serving someone, or while working towards any causes close to my heart. This gave my heart and soul the peace that I had always longed for, filling up the little vacuum of emptiness I felt for many years. This was also when I realized that in serving someone and doing something good for them, I was not only giving them my love, but, I was also loving myself in the process.

Having complete resonance and belief of inherent goodness and potential in every single human being propelled me to bring forth an idea that you now hold in your hands in the form of this book, The Happyness Bank. With extensive observations and research, it came to my awareness that today, only our bad deeds or *bad karma* if I should rightly put it, are physically recorded. Whether it is in the form of a newspaper articles, a social media post or even an FIR with the police. It seems more like a need for us to hold on to what is wrong, rather than focusing on what's right, and letting go.

This observation made me wonder, that if we could record our **GOOD DEEDS**, we would actually create a beautiful cycle of virtues that could motivate a person to do better, and carry forward the cycle of enacting those **GOOD DEEDS** . As I harped upon this thought while standing in the queue of a bank one day, a euphoric idea struck me. I felt inspired to create a passbook that would record all the **GOODNESS**, and **GOODNESS** alone! Most of us have grown up listening to tales from our elders that, all our actions are recorded by GOD, who sits right above us. "Well, they weren't entirely wrong," I smiled, and walked out of the bank.

THE Happyness Bank is a radical new concept, designed with the intention to create a lasting change in our lives, and also the lives of others around us. This simple yet powerful idea has been woven into a story which can help anyone look at life with a different perspective. A concept like this which has never been discussed on a global scale, is certain to have a significant effect on the collective consciousness of human race if implemented in a positive way.

The idea of having a Happyness Bank is to have a tangible system that **RECOGNISES**, **RECORDS**, and **REWARDS** all the **GOOD WORK** that one does. Practising this not only motivates us to do more good things by sharing what we have with others, but it also helps us lift our spirits in our darker days, when we feel down in the dumps. Life and its challenges can get to the best of us. The Happyness Bank is a medium that serves as a reminder to our inherent good nature or **GOD-SELF,** which we ALL possess.

Firmly believing that we are blessed with opportunities to carry out **GOOD DEEDS** at all times, I was introduced to Cyrus- a wonderful professor, and an acknowledged thought leader in the areas of Leadership and Management. He has also authored several best-selling books. Not only has Cyrus done a stupendous job in weaving together a story, but also helped me take my initiative forward. In Cyrus, I found a true person, who helped me develop my ideas, translating them into beautiful words, and ultimately giving the story a brilliant form.

THE Happyness Bank we believe, is **OUR** contribution to the world to make it a better and happier place to live in.

- **Vishal Gupta**

> The Happyness Bank I believe, is my
> contribution to the world to make it a better
> and happier place to live in.

"NEITHER FIRE NOR WIND,
BIRTH NOR DEATH CAN ERASE
OUR GOOD DEEDS."

– BUDDHA

Happÿness bank

> When there is great disappointment, we don't know if that's the end of the story. It may just be the beginning of a great adventure.
> – Pema Chodron

A New Beginning

'15 on the way to a wedding dead as their van rams into a train, at an unmanned railway crossing.'

'A chartered flight en-route the French Riviera crashes. 140 vacationers lose their lives'

'A bus carrying 22 pilgrims overturns on a steep road, killing them on the spot.'

'Terrorist attack at an upscale mall kills 16.'

The simple-hearted Atul Upadhay shook his head sadly as his eyes scanned through these tragic headlines, adorned on the front page of a newspaper in Mumbai. "Tragedy, tragedy, tragedy, all around!" he sighed, as he got up to carry on with the rest of the day. Atul was a humble soul, whole heartedly devoted to his family consisting of his wife and two teenaged children. He was the manager of a bank in Gauraj Nagar- a small town in the Pingaleshwar District, in Gujarat. Gauraj Nagar was not Atul's home-town. His bank had posted him there as an officer after his training period, and he eventually settled there with his family.

Atul was a very dedicated man. He progressed from the post of an officer to being the Branch Manager of the bank in Gauraj Nagar, with a small team of five people working under him. He had been working at this bank for the past twenty years, and his life consisted of nothing but a series of travelling from home to work, and back. He led a simple lifestyle, and also made a good husband and father. Atul would always refuse postings to other cities, which were a necessary corollary for a promotion to senior levels - a bank policy. This was solely because he valued the emotions he had for the small town and his family more than any other materialistic things.

The townspeople of Gauraj Nagar saw Atul and his family as one of their own. They recognised Atul as a good and friendly human being, someone who always had their best interests at heart. When people met him at the bank to discuss their financial affairs, he gave them honest advice, which came straight from the heart. He also always urged the townspeople to save and build a balance for the days when they would need it the most. "Who knows what the future will bring?" he would always say, smiling away at whoever came to him.

It was a quiet little town, Gauraj Nagar, with most of its five thousand inhabitants being from middle-class families. As it is with most small towns, people in Gauraj Nagar were quite social and maintained close knit relationships, sometimes gathering to celebrate festivals, or simply have a good meal at the eateries they loved.

On a pleasant Tuesday morning dawned in Gauraj Nagar, one could experience with all their senses, the normal hustle and bustle of a new day. Sounds of prayer bells accompanied by mantras; fragrances of all different kinds of food being prepared for loved ones, and the visual of fresh morning dew on the marigolds that almost every household had.

That particular Tuesday was going to change the lives of people in Gauraj Nagar, forever. As it is rightly said, *tragedy strikes when least expected*. Amidst the regular hustling and bustling of going to work and school, at 8.15 am, Mother Earth chose to open her arms wide, and strike an earthquake on 7.6 Richter scale, turning everything topsy-turvy within a matter of a few minutes.

Gigantic cracks appeared in the ground, swallowing up entire homes, men, and even cattle. The quake passed as quickly as it had announced its thunderous arrival, leaving the minds of the survivors numbed with shock, and their hearts wrenched with sorrow at the loss of their loved ones and

A New Beginning

possessions. Most of the humble little houses that once adorned the streets of Gauraj Nagar, were reduced to rubble. The roads were practically unusable, making assistance from volunteers possible only via a helicopter.

In today's fast paced and digitally advanced world, it doesn't take much time for things to go viral and spread on various different mediums. Within a matter of thirty minutes, news of the devastating earthquake in Gauraj Nagar was broadcasted across all news and radio in India.

When the earthquake had struck, Atul was on an official visit to Mumbai for two days, attending a conference. He leisurely went down from his hotelroom to the restaurant downstairs, to have his breakfast. "I can't wait to be back home," he said, smiling to himself.

Atul sipped on his freshly brewed coffee while looking around the restaurant. He noticed that the people seated there unusually glued to the TV there. He almost fell of the chair as he saw what was flashing with red headers on one of the news channels. An eartquake had hit his beloved town, Gauraj Nagar. Atul blanked out for a while, almost about to faint there and then in the restaurant. Somehow managing to handle his shaky self, Atul ran to his room, picked up his bags, and rushed in a cab to catch the first train available to the station nearest to Gauraj Nagar.

All Atul could think of in the train back to Gauraj Nagar was his family. He had tried to make several calls to his wife and friends but to no avail. Their phones were either switched off, or not reachable. "Where are they? Are they alive or dead? How will I get to them after reaching Gauraj Nagar?" he kept asking himself while crying profusely. Little did he know that the earthquake had already claimed the lives of his family.

> "It is not in the stars
> to hold our destiny but in ourselves."
> – William Shakespere

As he reached the station, the chaos he witnessed there made it evident that it had been a traumatic blow. The only mode of commute at this stage to Gauraj Nagar, five kilometres away from the station, was his feet. The quake had destroyed the road to an unimaginable extent. Atul walked and ran as fast as he could, managing to reach Gauraj Nagar in about an hour.

Atul collapsed upon reaching Gauraj Nagar. He couldn't believe what he saw in front of him. Complete devastation of homes and hearts alike. The visuals in front of him numbed him so much shock that he couldn't remember where his house was located. All the roads and landmarks leading towards it had vanished. After hours of searching, Atul managed to reach where his house once stood, only to find a pile of rubble instead of a building.

He asked whoever was around about his family that lived there. An old man seated close by told Atul that a few bodies were taken to the community centre, a while before he came. "It's all over!" he wailed as he made his way, walking as fast as he could to the community centre. On reaching there, he saw the bodies of his wife and children shoved into the corner of a large room, lying together with a hundred other corpses. He wept besides them for a while before performing their last rites, as did others who had lost their loved ones.

> *When everything has gone down,*
> *God wants you to look up."*
> *– Richmond Akhigbe*

In the days that followed the earthquake, the people of Gauraj Nagar made every possible effort to rebuild their broken homes and lives. Material assistance was provided by the authorities and common people across the country. Non-Government Organisations pitched in with as many volunteers as possible. Corporate houses as part of their Corporate Social Responsibility agendas dispatched food and clothes for the survivors. Pharmaceutical companies with a social bent of mind provided subsidised medicine and set up medical camps to tend to the injured, as the existing town hospital was neither prepared nor equipped to deal with such a cataclysmic disaster.

A New Begining

Happyness Bank

A New Begining

Within a month, all the volunteers left for their own home-towns or their next project, one by one. The townspeople were being collectively by professionals trained to handle such disastrous situations until then. Once these volunteers left, the townspeople had to work through their own personal debris by themselves, which was when the magnitude of their losses were felt even more deeply. The volunteers had helped with building new houses but it would probably never be sufficient enough to call it a home. Every family had lost at least one member, in some cases like Atul's, all. Even some of those that survived were too grievously injured to be of much help or support to the remaining members of their own family. A plethora of school going children had been orphaned, some of them escaping unscathed since they were on a picnic with their teachers outside Gauraj Nagar, on that catastrophic day.

> "Appreciate where you are in your journey,
> even if it's not where you want to be.
> Every season serves its purpose."

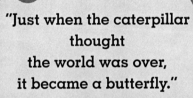

"Just when the caterpillar
thought
the world was over,
it became a butterfly."
– Proverb

Little Steps of Faith

Three months post the tragedy, most of the buildings in Gauraj Nagar had been reconstructed, yet the townspeople still struggled to get a grip on themselves emotionally. One would invariably find someone sitting outside their newly built house, wallowing in grief over the loss of their loved ones. It seemed like the entire town was covered in a smog making it almost impossible for them to find a ray of hope to move on with their lives. Everyone seemed to live on auto pilot mode, and felt no more than a lifeless vegetable.

Atul was equally battered emotionally. After all, his family was all that he had and he lived for them. He unknowingly found himself with tears rolling down his cheeks many a times, while doing mundane chores that his wife would usually do. He would often weep for hours post work, outside the school where his beloved children once studied. Coming home to an empty house without his wife's warm welcome and his children's giggles almost killed him alive. Atul also felt intense guilt for not being in town when the tragedy hit them. "I failed not only my family, but myself too. I was unable to protect my wife and children when they needed it the most!" he often said to himself, drowning himself in anger and resentment.

Atul found the courage and decided to read the newspaper on one of the Sundays. Reading the newspaper was a habit Atul's father had instilled in him since childhood, and he enjoyed it as well. Like everyone else in Gauraj Nagar, Atul had become skeptical about hearing or reading any more news, as the word news in itself would trigger traumatic memories and uncontrollable fear of losing what little was left. As Atul picked up the newspaper that afternoon, he hoped to read some light-hearted news and get some relief by reading positive developments which could have happened elsewhere in the world. To his dismay, he found that the news from other quarters of the globe were just as grim. Could it be that these newspapers simply specialised in publishing negative news? "No," he

thought to himself. He recalled that even when he had kept in touch with the outside world through different mediums, way before the earthquake had disoriented life, the news he read somehow managed to drain him emotionally. All the headlines ever shouted out was related to calamities-either natural, or man-made.

Atul, while browsing through the pages of the newspaper, read an article about walls being demolished at a Municipal school in Mumbai in order to widen roads. The razing took place during school hours, scaring most of the children inside the school premises. When a journalist questioned the Municipal officer in charge, as to how they could be so callous and conduct a demolition with children still in the school, the officer ruthlessly answered, "Why should I care? My children don't attend this school!"

Atul's heart sank once again. "Was there never going to be an end to the troubles human beings faced?" he thought to himself. As he blankly gazed at the newspaper, he couldn't help but think of what he could possibily do to help himself, and also the citizens of Gauraj Nagar. After all, he was a well-know and a respected part of the society. He was equally responsible to do something for the town where he lived and flourished for over two decades. Atul kept racking his brains as to how he could aid himself and others in overcoming the grief of the diaster that had hit the very core of their beings. Just like Atul, the townspeoples' lives also needed a gentle push to bring back their will to live. Moving on with life was now imperative.

As Atul started to fold the newspaper and place it aside, an article suddenly caught his eye. This article that was destined to change not only his life, but also the lives of people in Gauraj Nagar, India, and billions throughout the world. This article contained a seed which germinated in Atul's fertile mind, holding within it the potential to feed probably every human being on this planet.

> "Every adversity, failure and heartache, carries with it, the seed of an equivalent or a greater benefit."
> – Napoleon Hill

Little Steps of Faith

The article read-*The principal of Northland College, John Tapene, has offered a few words of wisdom from a judge who regularly deals with the youth. "We always hear the same cries from teenagers- What can we do? Where can we go?" the judge says. "The answer is simple- Go home, mow the lawn, wash the windows, lean to cook, build a raft, get a job, visit the sick, study your lessons and after you've finished, read a book. Your town does not owe you any recreational facilities and your parents do not owe you fun.*

The world does not owe you a living, YOU owe the world something. You owe it your time, energy and talent so that no one will be at war, in sickness and lonely again. In other words, grow up, stop whining and get out of your dream world. Develop a backbone and get rid of your wishbone. Start behaving like a responsible person. You are important and you are needed. You cannot sit around and wait for somebody to do something, someday. Someday is NOW and that somebody is YOU!"

"This is so true!" Atul said to himself, "The truth can often seem bitter. We cannot sit around feeling sorry for ourselves, when there is always someone who is worse off than we are, and needs more help than we do. We at least had volunteers helping us but I am sure there are people out there who had to rebuild their lives after losing their loved ones, all on their own. There is always something to be grateful for, no matter how bad in physical reality the situation seems to be."

Atul *found yet another uplifting article, that read- 'Two Sikh Men took off their turbans and used them as ropes, to pull out and save a few drowning youngsters. The turban is a very important religious symbol for the Sikhs, hence it is not an easy decision to make if it has to be taken off for any reason.'*

Atul read that same article over and over again, mouthing every syllable aloud, absorbing every word. As he lay the newspaper beside him, he faintly remembered a story he had heard repeatedly from his relatives as a child, about a young man that had suffered great personal loss. That man overcame his loss by immersing himself in social service. As this vague thought flittered through his mind, he realised that although he felt he had always been a good man at heart, never harming animals or people in thoughts, words, or deeds, he felt that he had not really done anything significant hat required effort or investment of his time and energy.

Atul began to experience a small shift within himself. He felt that he could involve himself in activities that would help him deal with the loss of his wife and children in a more constructive way. The option of another marriage was out of question for him since he was sure that no woman would ever be able to take the place of his devoted, late wife. Atul also realised that he was one of the lucky ones to have survived the calamity, hence, there was surely a reason for it.

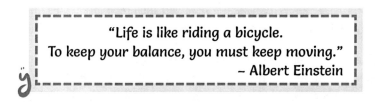

> "Life is like riding a bicycle.
> To keep your balance, you must keep moving."
> – Albert Einstein

Atul walked over to the window and stared at all the people making an effort to move on with their lives. "Make the entire town of Gauraj Nagar your family!" Atul heard a little voice from within himself. As this thought flashed and lit a bulb in his head, Atul realized that the townspeople had been like an extended family to him, all these years. Now was the time, Atul thought, to give back to the town and its people, in some way. Atul was convinced that the reason he was spared by the tragic earthquake, was because he was meant to do something for Gauraj Nagar and its people.

Upon realising the reason for him surviving the quake, Atul racked his brain for weeks together for an idea that could lift up the spirits of the sorrow-drowned townspeople. He knew that the town needed something more than money and mere theoretical hope. Something concrete had to be done. Something that would be welcomed with an open heart, and also motivate the townspeople to bring about a lasting change in their lives. A certain Buddhist theory often mentions that when you help others overcome their sorrows, the heavy baggage of sorrows you carry on your bag start falling off. We heal ourselves by helping others heal, and others heal when we heal ourselves.

As Atul's thoughts started shifting from the vague to the specific, his mind drifted him back in time, forty years ago from the present. He was seated near his grandmother's knee, eagerly listening to her pearls of eternal wisdom, "At school, you have a single and generalised subject of science. This shall later be split into three subjects once you reach the higher standards- Physics, Chemistry and Biology. Physics may be taught to you as a science, but remember, Physics has as much to do with spirituality as it has to do with science. A great scientist once said and proved - *Every action has an equal and opposite reaction. This is also known as KARMA in spiritual terms.* Ancient scholars who walked holy land who have left us with the message - *What you sow now, you shall reap later.* This knowledge is not just fascinating, but as practical as the laws of science.

Hence my child, never forget our ancient spiritual wisdom in the quest for scientific studies." Though not formally educated, Atul's grandmother had learnt how to read and write all by herself, eventually developing a deep fondness of reading.

A known fact that what one focuses on expands, Atul's thought and emotion processes had gradually started making a more empowering shift within himself, without him even consciously knowing it. An awareness dawned upon him that everything belonged to a SINGLE SOURCE from which everything emanates. He felt science and spirituality both belonged to that same SINGLE SOURCE. All spiritual practices and religious scriptures written thousands of years ago and read out in temples, were of at least as much importance, as the realities of science which are read in text books in schools and colleges today.

Reminiscing his grandmother's words continuously, Atul for the first time in three months inhaled some peace, and exhaled the burden of pain he had kept locked up in his heart. Not that he wanted to, but he had no possible method nor practical assistance to help him cope with the emotional downfall that he had experienced, together with the townspeople of Gauraj Nagar. Atul not only felt lighter from within, but also more energetic and aware of everything. He felt blessed to have a new found wisdom, at the precise time he needed it. That too from the source that he always felt was closest to his heart.

Atul believed that knowledge and wisdom expand when shared, hence he decided to share his thoughts with the townspeople in some way.

Especially with those who had drowned deep into sorrow. Of course, most of them knew the scriptures well being simple religious folk, but living in the modern era had reduced their knowledge to a theoretical mode, rather than letting them take a prominent place in an individual's life in practical sense.

> "You can only lose something that you have, but you cannot lose something that you are."
> – Ekharte Tolle

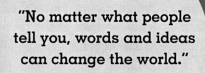

"No matter what people
tell you, words and ideas
can change the world."

- Robin Williams

A Silver Lining

Atul was eager to avail an opportunity to share his thoughts with the townspeople of Gauraj Nagar. He knew that almost every inhabitant of Gauraj Nagar would be gathered for a mass memorial service that would be held at a large ground, on the outskirts of town. This memorial service would be held in honour of all those who lost their lives in the gruesome earthquake. Atul being an important citizen of the town, was scheduled to be one of the speakers at the solemn occasion.

As Atul went to work the day before the memorial, he casually wondered if time in Gauraj Nagar would continue being measured from the date of the quake, just as the count of years in the English calendar is a representative of Jesus Christ's birth. Before he had the flashback to his childhood, Atul had thought of just sharing a few words of solace, comfort and hope at the memorial service. But now, with his newly found awareness and wisdom that helped Atul feel more at peace with himself and everything around him, inspired him to convey a lot more than mere hope.

As soon as Atul **stepped inside the bank,** he was told that two out of his **remaining** three team members had called in sick that **day, which** meant that he had to help out at the cashier's desk in addition to his **usual** managerial duties. As the day went **on,** Atul smiled and greeted the customers as they walked in to the **bank, either** to withdraw cash, or get their passbooks updated. Most of the townspeople had lost their passbooks **and other** important **official** documents **during** the quake. It was **going to be** a herculean task for them to get another set of identity papers **to get new** passbooks issued. Fortunately, the government had instructed the insurance companies and the bank to be humane in their approach, and not function in their usual bureaucratic manner. Also, the fact that bank account records were now stored electronically in a central database helped facilitate the process.

Atul holding a responsible position as the manager of the town bank, and Gauraj Nagar being a small town, he knew most of the customers personally. Hence, he had been requested to help out with identification of individuals to facilitate a fresh set of identity papers. **This activity** brought him even closer to the townspeople, as they now felt that **Atul** had helped them **in rebuilding** their lives by having displayed faith in their identities. That day was a busy one for Atul, hardly giving him any time to think of what he would say to the people of Gauraj Nagar the next day **at the** memorial service.

An early riser that Atul always was, he woke up at six the next morning and decided to go out for a walk. It seemed like a peaceful Sunday morning to him. As he looked around, he felt things had relatively settled down in Gauraj Nagar. Even though the roads and pavements looked almost normal once again, the town for some reason seemed dirtier than it was before the earthquake. He hypothesised that this could be because the townspeople had lost the will to live, let alone make the effort to clean their surroundings. They were going through the motions of life, mechanically; breathing, eating, working and sleeping. Their passion and enthusiasm were understandably missing.

On randomly asking a couple of people **around,** as to why everything seemed so dirty, Atul got similar answers from most of them. People feared the possibility of another quake striking at any **time, and** so, they did not see the benefit in keeping their surroundings up-to-date. *'Why make an effort when the outcome is uncertain'*, seemed to sum up the prevailing attitude.

Atul didn't like what he was seeing, yet he knew he couldn't clean up all the visible mess **all** by himself. He would need support if he really wanted to create a lasting change **in Gauraj Nagar and the lives of the townspeople. "I wonder how that will come about.** I hope I get some answers after the memorial service," he **said** to himself. Atul strongly believed that the memorial service would be the right platform to give the people of Gauraj Nagar a much needed push.

> "Winter always turns into spring."
> – Daisaku Ikeda

The townspeople of Gauraj Nagar assembled for the memorial service under the clear evening sky. Atul was seated on the podium together with three other respected and renowned citizens of Gauraj Nagar. The Principal of the local school, the Senior Inspector of the local police station, and the Head of the local municipality.

The Principal was the first to speak. She had tears in her eyes and a choke in her voice as she spoke about the umpteen number of children that had become orphans overnight. As of now, they were being looked after by relatives and neighbours. She had herself given shelter to three young children. But, how long could dutiful relatives and kind-hearted neighbours continue to do this? They had their own children to look after and their own mouths to feed. The townspeople were by and large not rich folk. Most of them were middle-class individuals, living respectable but hardly luxurious lives. No one supported the idea of sending those children away to an orphanage in the state capital. What was to be done? With no answers to her dilemma, the Principal expressed her concerns and walked back to her seat.

As the Senior Inspector took over the microphone, he expressed his concern at the increase in theft post the earthquake. As expected, it was to resort to robberies to tide themselves over this troubled period, it was neither acceptable, nor the solution to the problem. The government authorities had provided for food and clothing for the quake-affected, yet, a certain percentage of opportunists took advantage of the relaxed security and patrolling, as police personnel were still busy with the aftermath of relief-related work. The Inspector appealed to the people present, to work in unison to ensure their town overcome its misfortune in a healthy spirit of co-operation.

The Head of local municipality got up next and addressed the issue of the increasing amount of waste being dumped all around town. Although the personnel assigned to clean it were doing their job as best as they could, the townspeople had become lethargic about disposing waste at the designated bins and seemed to just drop waste wherever it was convenient. He appealed to the townspeople to stop the careless throwing around of waste, and reminded them that spoiling their once clean town was not the solution to get over their loss and depression. As he concluded his short speech and sat down, he could see that his words hadn't made much impact. People wanted practical solutions to overcome whatever they were going through and not long speeches and repeated condolences, which only added salt to their burning wounds.

As Atul stood up to talk next, he knew that the people gathered there had not been impressed with the previous three speakers so far. It was clearly visible on their faces and with their body language.

A lot of people had already started looking at their watches even before he uttered a word. All the brilliant thoughts that Atul had decided to share with the people of Gauraj Nagar, disappeared like fairy dust as his mind suddenly blanked out. He had never addressed such a large gathering before. All Atul did for a few moments was gaze at the thousand odd people assembled there, all with dejected looks on their faces.

> *"You cannot teach a man anything,*
> *you can only help him find it within himself."*
> *– Galileo*

Atul closed his eyes to say a small prayer, since he was shaking with fear from within. As he did that, an image of his grand-mother vaguely floated before his eyes. "Give them hope," he felt she said to him gently, "They need love and compassion. Guide them as I guided you through stories." As Atul opened his eyes, he felt instilled with a lot more confidence then before. He decided to speak from his heart, ans surrender the outcome of his speech to the Divine.

A Silver Lining

"My dear brothers and sisters of Gauraj Nagar," he began, fumbling a little out of nervousness, "Many years ago, you welcomed me into your hearts. I was new to this town then, and had arrived here newly-married with my wife. I have been pretty content since then. I had a loving wife, two adorable children, a stable job, a good house, and lovely friends like you all. I was pretty sure that the rest of my life was going to be as

happy and peaceful, until the quake hit Gauraj Nagar, and robbed me of
my family, just like most of you all present here. It has not been easy for
me to get over their loss and stand here to talk. I am still working towards
healing my wounded heart like every body else. The hope of seeing them
some day, in some other world keeps me alive and motivated."

A Silver Lining

Atul's words led to a huge and loud murmur amonst the crowd of the people. He felt he might not have been able to frame his words correctly. Just as he was thinking of what to do next, someone from the crowd called out in anger, "What on earth are you talking about? How do you know for sure that you will see them in another world? Do you really believe there is this other world you spoke about?

Do you even believe there is a God? If there is, why did He let this tragedy befall us? We have never harmed anybody as far as we are aware. Why have we been hurt so terribly? Why have our lives been torn apart so miserably?"This not only seemed like the voice of a single frustrated man, but probably expressed the anguish of almost every person gathered there.

Almost everyone in the crowd nodded their heads in agreement, and many added their sounds of approval. The people of Gauraj Nagar had always been simple God-loving people who would diligently perform their rituals and prayers, with the hope that the Gods they prayed to would protect them from any harm ever befalling them. Today, these people stood there feeling confused and betrayed. What indeed was Atul going to say that would bring some solace to their weary hearts and burdened souls?

Atul's mind by now had gone on an over-drive. "Maybe they think I have gone insane with the loss of my family," he thought to himself. He closed his eyes once again, took a deep breath and turned inwards to give an answer to his townspeople. In those split seconds that he stood mute on the stage, the tales he had heard from his grandmother long ago, flashed through his mind at the speed of light. THIS, he knew, was what the people of Gauraj Nagar needed to hear.

"Brothers and sisters," he began once again, humbly. "All of us standing here today have heard **of** the word **KARMA**. If you are Hindu, you would know that it is described in the *Atharva Veda as - 'Do not be led by others, awaken your own mind, amass your own experience.'* The Rig Veda further adds - *'One should perform karma for the benefit of humanity with an unbiased approach. Bias gives birth to evil, which creates thousands of obstacles in our path. The person who is always involved in good deeds experiences unceasing divine happiness.'*

The Sikh have been advised in the Guru Granth Sahibjin - *'I seldom end up where I wanted to go, but always end up where I deserve to be.'* It also says - *'Born because of karma of their past mistakes, they make more mistakes and fall into further trouble. According to the karma of one's past actions, one's destiny unfolds, even though everyone wants to be so lucky.'*

The Zoroastrian philosophy can also be summed up in six words - *'good thoughts, good words and good deeds.'*

The Jain Saint Mahavira has said—*'Just as you do not like misery, others also do not like it either. Knowing this, you should do unto them what you want them to do unto you.'* He also advised that our growth consists not merely in an increase of ideas, but also in our capacity to feel for others in a million and one ways.

The Bible of the Christians says - *'Do not be deceived. God is not mocked, for whatever one sows, that he shall also reap.'*

Islam *has the concept of Kirafah - 'What you give, you will get it back; whether good or bad.'*

The Taoists texts of the wise Chinese give hope to those who wish to repent - *'If one has indeed done any deed of wickedness, but afterwards alters his way and repents, resolved not to do anything wicked, but to practice dedicatedly all that is good, he is sure in the long run to obtain good fortune: - this is called CHANGING CALAMITY INTO BLESSING.'"*

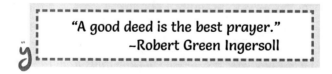

> **"A good deed is the best prayer."**
> –Robert Green Ingersoll

As all these words flowed with Divine ease from Atul's mouth, **while** the crowd there stood **frozen,** trying to make sense of every word that he said. "So yes, my dear brothers and sisters," he continued, "What has happened to us is not a random act of nature. As much as nature has its ways, it never really does anything with the intention of being cruel. There are umpteen examples of this all around us, only if we make an effort to focus on that. Do we not sleep soundly with the gentle breeze that Nature provides **us** in abundance? Do we not quench our thirst with water? Do we not fill our stomachs and get **the** much needed energy by biting into the sweet fruits that Mother Nature gives us throughout the year?

"**Look** around yourselves my friends. Do we not take shade below the green, leafy trees, when the mid-day Sun has grown too hot for our bodies to handle? Why then are we blaming Mother Nature for this earthquake? Why have we forgotten to appreciate all these great gifts of Nature, without which you and I would not be standing here today? Yes, I say **GIFTS**. For Mother Nature expects no payment for any of these things. Yet, see how we have been acknowledging her. Being grateful for all that we already have seeming to be a far-fetched reality.

"**Filth** surrounds our roads and our entire town, only because most of us are too lazy to look for a dustbin. Plastic bags fly around choking innocent animals. The river which flows near our town is **also** crying **with the** pollutants our chemical plants are pouring into it, day and night. We are cutting down trees as if there is no tomorrow, without bothering to plant new ones to replace them. How is the ecological system meant to function normally like this?"

"**Let** us not blame a benevolent God or Mother Nature. If at all we have anyone to blame, it is only OURSELVES. What we are going through today, dear friends, is of our own making. What we see happening to us on the outside today, is merely a reflection of what is going on within ourselves. This is nothing but a reciprocation of our own deeds, done intentionally or unintentionally, across lifetimes. Recall what the great sage Chanakya wrote in his classic work, *Chanakya Neeti*, many ages ago - *'Poverty, diseases, conflicts, and other problems are nothing but the fruits from the tree of one's own misdeeds.'*"

As Atul's words were passionately flowing from his heart, an irritated voice emerged from the crowd, "How do we believe what you say?" he asked, "If we had lived lifetimes before this, would we not remember them? What proof do we have that our good and bad deeds are being recorded? It's not as though there is a **'BANK OF KARMA' that** issues us a passbook or something!" he added, sarcastically.

Atul smiled warmly, and responded, "Do we not often feel that we have done little or no wrong, until the one who felt wronged by us brings it to our awareness? Similarly, we unintentionally forget the good we have done to others, however insignificant we may logically think it is. Just as the wrong we could have done comes back to us in form of calamities and different kinds of life lessons, our good deeds also get reciprocated, all in due course of time. God has a perfect record of every drop of rain, that has fallen on every leaf, since the beginning of time."

Just as Atul uttered these words, a brainwave that was destined to change the very face of humanity on this planet, struck him. After all being a banker all his life, he knew about the passbook system of entering debit and credit to perfection. "Actually, just as this gentleman has rightly suggested, why don't we initiate a **'BANK OF GOOD KARMA'?**" he asked the crowd, "After all, as humans we love tangible things, and need proof before believing in anything.

Holding a **GOOD DEED PASSBOOK** in our hands, that would hold a record of all the good work and deeds that we carry out, would motivate and inspire us to do even more good."

Atul's intention was not to act as judge, but rather, inspire and motivate the people of his town to collectively overcome the misery that had over-cast them. Atul made up his mind, in that moment itself, to create a **GOOD DEED PASSBOOK**. As he officially declared the initiation of the passbook to the crowd standing in front of him,

Atul further added that the passbook would not have anything negative included in it. Only the **GOOD DEEDS**. This passbook would help people acknowledge and appreciate good work, by simply recording and recognising them. It would also act as a solace whenever someone was going through a difficult phase, and feeling low.

Atul had no doubt that it was only the voice of the **Divine** that could have spoken through him, as he stood on the stage inspired and confident. The seed of a simple passbook, as a means of giving people hope to overcome a personal tragedy, germinated into the most potent force to harness the supreme **POWER OF GOODNESS,** that this planet could

48

have ever witnessed. This simple **GOOD DEED PASSBOOK** concept which Atul promised the audience in a spur of a moment, within a short span of time, went on to become more practically beneficial to mankind, than all the organised religions put together.

> "Nothing is as potent a force as an idea whose time has come."

Happÿness
bank

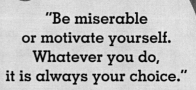

"Be miserable
or motivate yourself.
Whatever you do,
it is always your choice."

- Wayne Dyer

Committed
to
Transform

**hen** will we get our Passbooks and who will issue them to us? What type of good deeds would be recorded?" came the eager questions from the enthused audience. "Do not worry my dear ones. You shall be guided through the process in due course of time," replied Atul, getting away from the dais and thereby ending the programme. The Principal, the head of municipality and the head of the town police, looked questioningly at Atul. This surely was not the agenda for the evening. They seemed visibly miffed with Atul, for committing something so vague and unheard of to the entire town, without first consulting them.

As the function came to an abrupt end, almost the entire crowd rushed on stage to get a hold of Atul, firing him with a million questions all at once. After a hundred days of sadness, the townspeople saw a **SILVER LINING** lying hidden somewhere after living in days of perpetual darkness and sorrow. Atul's idea surely seemed to have hit the bull's eye- the hearts of the townspeople.

The commitment he had made to the entire town had been purely spontaneous. As Atul pondered over what he had said on the way back home, he panicked. How would he, who had known nothing but banking all his life, produce a **GOOD DEED PASSBOOK** for an entire town? As he racked his brains over how to now proceed, he yet again recalled all that his grandmother had told him in her own simple language, of how the Lord had made this Universe and all within. How much the Lord loved to see His children happy. She had also told him that the Lord never desired to see any of His children miserable. Whatever miseries and sorrows we thought we faced were only to make us better and stronger, even though we may not recognise them as such in the midst of a problem. "**A GOOD DEED PASSBOOK** will be arranged somehow," he assured himself as he drifted off to sleep.

> "Good deeds is the only valid currency in the hereafter,
> so try to earn as much as you can."

Early the next morning, Atul invited a few town elders to the bank to discuss the practical details of getting together a **GOOD DEED PASSBOOK**. As all the invitees gathered and settled down in his cabin, they faced Atul expectantly and started questioning him almost immediately, "What exactly did you mention yesterday?" asked Mr. Shastri, a small factory owner who manufactured bottle-caps. He too had lost his wife in the tragedy.

"Yes, you've brought some hope to our lives again, however vague. We pray there is some substance to whatever you had said," added Mr. Dev, a Chartered Accountant.

"Patience, Sir," said Atul, "I will be honest with all of you. When I spoke of the idea on stage, it was just a thought that struck me at that moment in time.It was merely something to comfort everyone present, just the way a mother comforts a sobbing child. Although the idea is still vague and hazy, I strongly believe that there could be something that can be built from it.

"Credit for whatever I am now about to tell you, If you find it to be of any value, goes to my beloved grandmother. It is she who ingrained in me since childhood, the love for the Divine. She told me tales of Gods and Goddesses, of reincarnation, karma, and of the world that lies beyond. Most expressly, she told me how bad begets bad and good begets good. Nothing in this Universe happens by chance and that nothing is random. It may sound like the rambling of an old woman, until you recall that one of the greatest scientists, Albert Einstein, also said something very similar when he mentioned, *'God does not play dice.'"*

As a wave of loud whispers ran over the room, Atul turned the attention back to him**self** and continued, "Although I shall need all your help and valuable inputs, the objective is one, and one alone. Our town for whatever reason was hit by a terrible tragedy. We have suffered the loss of not only our **priced possessions** but also our livelihood. Though this kind of loss can be overcome almost entirely in time with financial help coming from **various** different trusts and government funds, the void that lies within each one of us cannot be filled with monetary aid alone. I do know that hearts are still aching from the loss of **their** loved ones. This **is** because most of us have not yet fully accepted and understand why this mighty, unforeseen tragedy has struck **on us** in the first place.

"**I** too have suffered as everyone else, I will not deny. The loss of my wife and children hurts me till date. What greater wealth can a man lose? Trust me when I say this, I have been equally shattered. If there is anything that has given me solace and the strength to stand here today, it is only my conscious effort, day in and day out, to change my perspective of life. Shifting focus on possibilities and solutions has not only made me accept my loss a lot more quickly, but also helped me learn a great lesson- '*Suffering happens by choice, and not by chance.*'

> "A single act of kindness throws out roots in all directions, and the roots spring up and make new trees.
> – Amelia Earhart

"**The** people of Gauraj Nagar need a lot more than mere comforting with philosophical words. They need to know that no matter what challenges they may face in their lives, they have their cushion of good deeds in the form of a little passbook **with them at all times**. All the answers that they seek outside of themselves shall come from within, as soon as they focus their **attention** on the victories they have **achieved,** instead of the challenges that they have faced."

By now, Atul had all the people seated in his cabin hooked onto his words. They heard him out intently without any interruption. They had no idea whatsoever as to how this inconsequential looking bank manager could possibly help in cushioning the blows of fate. Atul had never pitched anything in his life except bank accounts. As he paused for a few seconds and glanced at the expressions on everyone's faces, he understood that they were all clueless about what to do next. Speak.

Atul took a deep breath and began to explain once again, "I propose we start something called **THE BANK OF GOOD KARMA.** Wait, wait hear me out," he interjected, as he could see protests forming on the lips of those present, "It will not be a bank in the traditional sense. There shall be **NO MONETARY TRANSACTION**, but there shall surely be a passbook. **THE GOOD DEED PASSBOOK.** Every single person in Gauraj Nagar, including children, shall have an account with this bank and have their own passbook. A summary of all the good deeds that each account holder has accumulated shall be personally credited into this passbook, which shall stand in his or her name."

"You, Dev-*saahab*," Atul turned towards the chartered accountant, deciding to now involve the people gathered, "Can you kindly enlighten us with the basic concepts of accountancy and book-keeping?" "Well," Mr. Dev began with a small cough, not knowing exactly what Atul wanted to hear, "Accountancy is nothing but the recording of all our financial transactions. For example, if I buy some furniture for my business, I will have to record the money which I have used to pay for it, and also record the furniture as an asset **that** I shall possess."

"Excellent!" smiled Atul. "I suggest an additional passbook to be provided to all the townspeople, similar to the traditional bank passbook that they already have," he proposed. "We can have **BANK OF GOOD KARMA** written in a simple manner on the cover page, and record every good deed, however small, inside the passbook. Whether it is helping someone in distress, or cleaning up the pavement, people can come to us and tell us what they have done. We, as authorised personnel shall record all their good deeds for them in their passbook, thereby making it look official. I once again repeat, this will reaffirm belief in a person, that the goodness he has done is not lost to the wind.

Committed to Transform

> "What we do for ourselves dies with us. What we do for others and the world remains and is immortal."
> – Albert Pine

"**When** one feels low, he or she can always flip through their passbook and acknowledge that the world has been a better place because they live in it. Also, this record of goodness will serve as a reminder to individuals, that their good deeds are being recorded here in physical reality as they are in the Ultimate, Universal Databank. Most people prefer something tangible if they are to believe in it.

"**As** much as our brilliant Vedanta philosophy teaches us about concepts which are the very bedrock of life, not everyone is at that stage of spiritual evolution where they would be able to understand these intangible concepts, without some physical fulcrum to focus upon. This is also why we have idols and images of various Divine Beings. Vedanta philosophy itself says that the Divine has no form, but the common man cannot think in such a way. It is beyond his logical mind.

"**What** exactly constitutes a good deed is our call, collectively. This is precisely the reason why I have invited you all **here** today. I humbly request you to help me prepare a list consisting of all types of good deeds that we could record for the **townspeople,** in their **GOOD DEED PASSBOOK.** The very objective of this passbook is to not only make people feel good about themselves, but also to appreciate all the blessings they have received in different forms in their lives, till date. As someone rightly put it – *'the good we do is merely the rent we pay for our stay here on earth.'*"

> "You have to grow from the inside out.
> None can teach you, none can make you spiritual.
> There is no other teacher but your own soul."
> – Swami Vivekananda

"**If** this bank you propose is to represent the force of KARMA in a physical sense, shouldn't the bad or negative deeds also be recorded?" asked Mr. Dev, inquisitively. Atul smiled and replied, "I repeat. The purpose of this entire exercise is to motivate our people in these troubled times, and make them realise that there is hope. We should not under any circumstances burden our fellow townspeople with more bad memories. We solely want them to focus on the good that they have done or shall do in the future. Let us simply **RECOGNISE** and **RECORD** the good, and hand over the passbook back to its owner. Another thing I am certain of is that, our people, through helping one and another, shall be able to get over their own sorrows with much more ease."

"**Respected** elders, together with your approval for this idea, I also seek your valuable insights and suggestions on taking this initiative **ahead**. We shall need to raise some funds initially to provide people with their **GOOD DEED PASSBOOKS**. I shall **also** need your assistance in volunteering to update the **GOOD DEED PASSBOOKS**, as and when the townspeople approach us. It is not going to be daunting, please don't worry. All we have to do is update their passbooks with whatever good they have done in a structured format, once a week. As we formulate a list of good deeds, it will give **the townspeople a** direction **on** what type of good deeds can get a positive entry passed in their passbooks."

The invited guests who had gathered in Atul's cabin were fully convinced by now that he had come up with a brilliant idea. They also had faith in Atul's words. The discussions and deliberations between the wise men that had gathered in Atul's cabin thus began. Each of them had a different perspective on what constituted **as a** good deed.

They decided to work backwards rather than forward, identifying the major issues the town had, what kind of good deeds could minimise, and gradually eliminate these problems. After all, as we already know, *'People expect the state to do everything for them, but, the state has its limitations. Any genuine improvement is always brought about by the efforts of its interested citizens. Change begins with us.'*

Committed to Transform

> "You must be the change you want to
> see in the world."
> – Mahatma Gandhi

Atul encouraged everyone to jot down and share all that they thought was necessary, for the town to get back at its efficient best once again. The doctor present there spoke about the need for better hygiene management in order to prevent the spread of communicable diseases. He requested for help in the form of volunteers, at the town hospital. The heads of all religious institutions that had been called for the meeting, suggested programmes for people to update and implement their spiritual knowledge. This would foster peace amongst each other, thereby reducing conflict and even lower the crime rate. The Senior Inspector agreed with this whole-heartedly. The school Principal suggested the addition of a structured syllabus that included yoga, meditation and prayers. All of them also discussed the need to eradicate social evils such as child labour, child-marriage, and child abuse.

> "The best way to forget your own pain
> is to help ease the pain of another."
> – Unknown

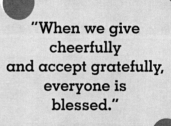

"When we give
cheerfully
and accept gratefully,
everyone is
blessed."

– Maya Angelou

Reaping Benefits

It took five hours for those gathered with Atul to shortlist all their ideas and put them onto a piece of paper. After much editing, two holistic lists were produced, that could aid the town in making it a better place.

LIST ONE contained information of all the current good activities and events that were currently scheduled in Gauraj Nagar. By reading this, the townspeople were made **to be** aware of **all** the good activities that would be taking place in town, where they were being held, and for how many days they would be conducted for. People could thus choose to participate in the activities that interested them.

For example, a sample of **LIST ONE** *for a particular day looked as follows:*

LIST ONE

- Yoga camp organised by Mr. Rasik Doshi from 6 a.m.
- Blood donation camp at Mahavir Hospital on 23rd, 24th, 25th, and 26th June
- Satsang at Mr. Ramniklal Jain's house on 23rd and 27th, from 6 p.m. to 7:30 p.m.
- Tree/Sapling planting activity on 27th and 28th – Assemble at town square at 9 a.m.
- Volunteers required to clean courtyard of Mahavir Hospital
- Volunteers required to provide lunch for Mr. Alvin D'Souza's family, whose wife is currently in hospital. Care for their child aged three is also required, till Mrs D'Souza recovers.
- Female volunteers required to escort girl-students from Gandhi School, back to their respective houses, post 4 p.m.

LIST TWO contained information of general and long-term activities, which a person could undertake to get his **GOOD DEED PASSBOOK** updated.

*A sample of **LIST TWO** looked as follows:*

LIST TWO

- Constructing a toilet in their own house, if not already existing.
- Volunteering / Assisting in the construction of a public toilet, in one's neighbourhood.
- Adopting a stray animal.
- Installing a dustbin outside one's Shop / Home.
- Enrolling for substance de-addiction programmes.
- Signing up for organ donation upon death.
- Ensuring polio and other necessary immunizations are given to all small children.
- Ensuring all the children in the family attend school, especially the girl child.
- Ensuring that marriage of girls only takes place after they are 18 years of age.
- Volunteering for town security on a rotational basis
- Academic Mentoring / Coaching of school children
- Assisting illiterate people with their bank, insurance, medical paperwork

This is how the initial two lists of good deeds were formulated, and eventually distributed to every single person in Gauraj Nagar. A simple design was made for the passbooks, which the town printer offered to print for the entire town, at a subsidised rate. The funds for these acts were provided willingly, by a couple of businessmen in town. For them, this went on to be recorded as their first good deed.

An envelope containing the very first **GOOD DEED PASSBOOK,** a note explaining why it is being distributed and the corresponding **GOOD DEED LIST,** was distributed to every individual of Gauraj Nagar. The townspeople were informed via the note and through the distributors of the envelopes that they could come at certain specified times in a week, and get their **GOOD DEEDS** entered into the passbook by the authorised panel. A structured system which prioritised the requirements of those in need, was also collated. This data was then provided to the entire town in the form of two lists every morning, put up on the town square notice board.

Atul and the town elders were very happy with all that they had come up with, yet, at the back of their minds, they were equally worried. "What if the motivation fades away after this initial euphoria? What if people just forget everything all of a sudden, making all our efforts go in vain?" they discussed amongst themselves. It was only human to have such doubts. After all, we can neither change anyone, nor can we influence anyone's choice. Luckily, as the **GOOD DEED** scheme was put into action, Atul's doubts had been proved wrong. The response and the resulting change with the implementation of the **GOOD DEED PASSBOOK** had surpassed all of Atul's expectations, way beyond description.

One of the positive impacts that Atul's scheme resulted in, was the steep reduction of crime rate in Gauraj Nagar. Those who had committed crimes in the past, found a reason to mend their previous ways and lead a better life filled with dignity. Some individuals previously known to be stone cold with their attitude towards others, suddenly started showing a positively different side of their nature.

The girl children of Gauraj Nagar were now safely escorted to and from school by mothers volunteering their time for escort duty, again on rotation basis. Those parents who had withdrawn their children from school, most of them being girls, once again had their children admitted. The girls were furthermore encouraged to finish their college and graduation instead of sitting at home.

The literate population volunteered to coach sons and daughters of their not-so-fortunate neighbors. As a result, these children started securing better grades at school, and took a keener interest in their studies. These individuals also formed volunteer groups to help adults who could not read and write. They helped them learn basic literacy skills and also assist with their bank paperwork, reading electricity bills, etc. Letters were also read and written on behalf of them.

Religious heads of all faiths got together to conduct lectures for the townspeople and special lectures for the children. Stories were narrated from all religious texts, which collectively highlighted the goodness prevalent in the teachings of every religion. This fostered harmony amongst all, at levels beyond imagination. The Hindus, for example, hosted an *Iftaar* dinner every day of *Ramadan*, for their fellow Muslim friends. The Muslims avoided eating meat in public places, during any of the important Hindu festivals. Some Sikh citizens sponsored the maintenance of the churches, with the deed being reciprocated by their Christian brothers in the form of a sponsored *Langar* at the *Gurudwara*.

Individuals who had certain marketable skills started conducting workshops on holidays and Sunday mornings. This aided some of the under-privileged adults to learn a trade, become self-sufficient, and ultimately set up their own small-scale businesses.

It seemed that people had just been waiting for a sign to tell them where to begin and how to change their lives for the better. Challenges were always going to be present, but with their new found perspective and immense strength, Atul hoped that the people would be able to overcome them with much more ease and grace.

> "Something very beautiful happens to people when their world has fallen apart. A humility. A nobility.
> A higher intelligence emerges
> at just the point when our knees hit the floor"
> – Marianne Williamson

Gauraj Nagar, from being an ordinary small town, changed into a model town filled with love, peace and happiness, **almost** miraculously. Atul was **beyond** happy, as his idea which was born out of wild imagination, had finally seen fruition. He also told the people of Gauraj Nagar that the list of good deeds was not intended to be a static one. Anyone could suggest good deeds that could be added to the existing list, if deemed fit.

The **GOOD DEED PASSBOOK** had truly motivated the townspeople to make a conscious effort, to do and focus on the good.

'GOOD' Deed Pass Book

Account No. 25783

'GOOD' Name: Sarita Patel

Address: Room No.2, Panalal Terraces

Contact No.

Date	Description of the 'GOOD' Deed	Signature
24/8	Attended Yoga Camp	
18/9	Escorted girl students	
	to school	
29/9	Cleaned Mahavir Hospital	

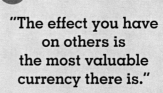

"The effect you have
on others is
the most valuable
currency there is."

– Jim Carrey

Questioning Goodness

Police Commissioner Arvind Desai wore a puzzled look on his face, as he flipped through the pages of Gauraj Nagar's crime report. The report was prepared by his subordinate, Inspector Shivlal Nayee. Arvind Desai was a stickler for proper paperwork, believing it to be the first step to build an efficient organisation, and also control crime. He prided himself with heading a district where crime rates were relatively low in almost all towns that came under him. Amongst the various towns which came under Arvind Desai's jurisdiction, Gauraj Nagar had always been one with a crime record slightly on the higher side. This could be attributed to multiple factors such, multiple religious communities occupying the town, which had often led to communal clashes; the average resident being less literate than his counterparts in other towns, and the lack of employment opportunities for the residents.

As Commissioner Desai browsed through the reports, he was sure that Shivlal had erred in his paper work, tremendously. The crime graph of the last quarter in Gauraj Nagar showed the crime rate as an unbelievable zero! "How could this be?" Commissioner Desai asked himself, flabbergasted with what he was seeing, "Shivlal has always been careless with his paperwork. This could be a result of that!" The Commissioner called Shivlal at once, preferring to tell him off in person.

Shivlal on the way to Commissioner Desai's cabin, wondered what had gone wrong as he hadn't been told why he was called for so urgently. Deep down in his heart, he was sure he was going to get a firing, since he was well versed with the volatile temper of his boss. "Oh Dear Lord! Please save me from the wrath that awaits me!" he prayed silently as he entered Commissioner Desai's cabin, with trembling knees.

As soon as the Commissioner's eyes caught Shivlal standing in front of him, he roared loud enough for the entire police station to hear, "What nonsense have you given me?

Why are your reports so erroneous? Do you not know simple English and Maths? Are you so dumb and inexperienced that you cannot investigate and record something as simple as a crime rate? When will you ever not make a mistake in your life?" The Commissioner threw the crime reports of Gauraj Nagar on the floor as he stormed out of his cabin to answer his phone.

Shivlal, barely able to catch his breath, gathered the papers that were scattered all over the room. As he was arranging them chronologically, he quickly browsed through them, wondering what grave mistake he had made. What was the Commissioner talking about? He was sure that he had checked Gauraj Nagar's crime reports at least three times before submitting them.

Questioning Goodness

"Stop flipping through those pages and tell me about the nonsense you have presented me with! You very well know I cannot tolerate mistakes, especially when it comes to paperwork and crime reports!" howled Commissioner Desai as he walked back into the cabin. "Forgive my audacity, Sir, but what part of the crime report would you be referring to?" asked Shivlal in a meek voice, shaking with even more fear. "How and why does the crime rate of Gauraj Nagar show a zero? On what basis have you tabulated this? Have you messed up while entering the figures or are things so bad that you are trying to hide the real picture? Have you started taking bribes from criminals to suppress the actual figures? How can there not be a single crime in three months? ANSWER ME!" yelled Commissioner Desai, at the top of his voice.

Shivlal's fears comparatively reduced after all that the Commissioner had said. He was expecting a counter check on the figures that he had presented, just not in the way Commissioner Desai had brought it out. As genuine as these figures were, Shivlal had been puzzled himself while tabulating them. He knew Gauraj Nagar had never until the earthquake, even closely reflected such a low crime rate, let alone it being completely nil. In fact, he had actually expected it to be higher, considering the fact that the town had just been through a major tragedy. It is common under such circumstances for the crime rates to soar up.

"Sir, if you are referring to the fact that the crime figures are zero, I share your surprise. I can assure you though, there is no error. These are the actual figures. I personally double-checked them before preparing the reports and sending them to you, as I know how particular you are about such matters," Shivlal blurted, in an attempt to placate his boss. "But how can this be?" asked the Commissioner, in a slightly softer tone, realising that he shouldn't have blasted Shivlal without asking for a valid explanation first.

> "When surrounded by day to day issues, there is a tendency to forget the good things we are bestowed with."
> – Dr. A.P.J Abdul Kalam

Observing a small shift in the Commissioner's behavior, Shivlal immediately took the opportunity to explain, just in case the Commissioner erupted once again, "Well, sir, it is like this. You are absolutely right in doubting these figures, because being away from the ground realities of the new Gauraj Nagar, no one can possibly imagine the change that has taken place in the town over the last few months."

Shivlal continued in flattery mode, "Sir, you are very observant. Your achievements speak for themselves and I know you shall soar higher. Even though you have so many towns under your jurisdiction, sitting here in Keshav Nagar away from the scene of action, you have identified even the minutest of details, simply by glancing at figures on a paper." Shivlal knew that even though his boss would tell him to shut up and stop praising him, inwardly he would be soaking up the flattery with a childlike delight.

He was sure his gambit had worked because the Commissioner could barely conceal the delight on his face. "Get to the point now, Nayee," smirked the Commissioner.

"Well, Sir," went on Shivlal, "I was posted in Gauraj Nagar a while before the earthquake struck there. At that time, I did a thorough investigation of the place. I also managed to get the history of the crime situation there, and was told about the known troublemakers in the vicinity from my predecessor. In terms of crime, Gauraj Nagar was just like any other average town of its size in modern India. It had its share of thefts, communal clashes, molestation issues, etc. People in mega-cities feel that crime only exists in their cities, and rural areas are a peaceful oasis of calm. But, as police personnel we are aware that such is not the case. In fact, there is a higher incidence of crime in certain small towns than in mega - cities, maybe because of multiple socio - economic cultures, lack of literacy, and so on."

"Sir, the point is, I am myself puzzled at the recent change that has occurred in Gauraj Nagar, as far as the lack of crime is concerned. Of course, it's a good thing, but if this trend continues, most of us would soon be out of jobs!" giggled Shivlal, attempting to inject a spot of humour into the proceedings, but seeing the Commissioner's stony face, he rapidly continued with a factual narrative. "Sir, the only event I can associate this

Questioning Goodness

sudden drop in crime with is, some new scheme that the bank manager there has introduced, about six months ago," said Shivlal, being unsure himself on how Atul's scheme worked.

As a policeman, and being more used to the negative side of human behavior, Shivlal was not attuned to understand the power of positivity, and how an entire town could be motivated to do only good things. The Commissioner sat up straight on hearing this. "What new scheme?" he queried, "Is the local bank of Gauraj Nagar offering a higher rate of interest than banks in other places? Are the townspeople now more well off as a result, and has this led to the drop in crime?"

"No, no, Sir," Shivlal replied, "It has nothing to do with higher interest rates. Only the Government has the authority to do that." "I know that, silly guy!" snapped the Commissioner, "If it's not to do with interest rates, then what is it? Actually, all I'm interested to know is the connection between this so called scheme and a nil crime rate," said the Commissioner, getting agitated once again.

"You haven't taken to drinking, have you?" he quizzed Shivlal, "You submit fantastically low crime figures for a town that you are in-charge of. Then, you talk some half-witted nonsense about these low figures having to do with some hare-brained scheme which the bank manager of the town has initiated. Be clear and think before you speak!" the Commissioner barked once again, with his irritation soaring up.

Shivlal was dumbfounded. "What exactly did that idiotic bank manager initiate?" he asked himself. He wished he had paid more attention to Atul's scheme while investigating, in order to answer his ever erupting boss. But **then**, Shivlal, like most policemen, had little time for the intricacies of the human mind, especially when they weren't pointing in a negative direction. Just like every person working with the law, he was trained to suspect every motive of a human being- to keep a tab on the slightest trace of likely criminal behavior.

It is a sad fact that we can only see what we are consciously trained to look out for. If we look only for the bad, we cannot recognize the good even if it passes under our very nose. If we expect the worst from people, the worst is what we get. While this may be an essential part of police training- viewing everyone with suspicion and operating on the principle that everyone is guilty till proved innocent, and believing that most people are sinners at heart, is a philosophy that hardens one's soul, and does little good to people around us as well.

> "Don't tell people how to do things. Tell them what to do and let them surprise you with their results."
> – George S. Patton

Shivlal racked his brain further, as he still had no concrete answer to Commissioner Desai's questions. If he didn't answer, he was sure that the Commissioner would pounce on him once again. Having kept his ears open in Gauraj Nagar, Shivlal had managed to pick up certain terms such as **'THE GOOD DEED PASSBOOK'** and **'THE GOOD DEED LIST'**. As soon as he remembered these phrases, he immediately made an attempt to explain to the Commissioner once again.

"Sir," he said, mustering up as much courage as he could, to explain, "That bank manager in Gauraj Nagar has started some nonsense about **KARMA & GOOD DEEDS,** and is making people believe in doing good things.

I believe the impact of the low crime rate is due to the increased efficiency of our police force and their vigilant patrolling which I insisted upon, post the earthquake. Knowing that the disaster would lead to increased crime, I proactively ensured that we crack down on crime, and it has shown results," Shivlal beamed, heaving a sigh of relief as he finally managed to provide what he thought was a suitable answer.

"Hmmmph," grunted the Commissioner, not quite sure what to believe, "Maybe Shivlal is not lying. He surely wouldn't lie so blatantly," he thought to himself. Deciding to be double sure, the Commissioner instructed Shivlal to carry out another investigation in Gauraj Nagar, and report back in detail about the **GOOD DEED** madness there.

Shivlal was even more perplexed now as to how he was going to proceed. "Sir, under what section of the Indian Penal Code should I investigate this 'good-deed business?" Shival asked, innocently. He was accustomed to conduct investigations for offenses which had various sections dedicated to crimes ranging from theft and molestation to rape and murder. This new order to investigate **GOODNESS** left him dazed, as he was clueless about how to proceed. The Commissioner clenched his teeth at this question and yelled, "There is **NO SECTION** for this you fool! Just go and investigate all that you have been yapping about!"

Shivlal, deciding to be honest and also to avoid making it look like he was constantly erring in his work, responded, "Sir, I have only been trained to investigate crimes and offenses. I have not been given any training to observe, understand and report **GOODNESS.** I am only familiar with the bad stuff. I am sorry Sir, but I really don't know how to proceed with this investigation."

The Commissioner realized that even though Shivlal was partly right, asking him to investigate this case could turn out to be futile and possibly even counter-productive. As much as he disliked it, he decided that the only option he now had was to investigate this case himself by going to Gauraj Nagar, even if it meant doing it as an undercover cop.

> "How far that little candle throws his beams!
> So shines a good deed in a weary world."
> – William Shakespeare

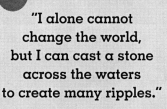

"I alone cannot
change the world,
but I can cast a stone
across the waters
to create many ripples."

– Mother Teresa

Proof of
the Truth

Commissioner Desai reached Gauraj Nagar the next morning, *incognito* - without his official vehicle or retinue accompanying him. Clad in plain clothes with dark sunglasses, he took an auto rickshaw to a guest house that he had booked in Gauraj Nagar. "I am determined to find out the reality of this zero crime rate and I shall!" he said to himself with conviction, as his journey to Gauraj Nagar began.

After checking in as Mr. Shastri and freshening up in his room, the Commissioner wandered out on to the streets of Gauraj Nagar, curious to roam the town where no crime had been reported in the last three months. He noticed almost instantly that the town looked much cleaner than when he had last been there, just post the earthquake. *Paan*-stains - the bane of almost every Indian town, were conspicuous by their absence. A couple of new public toilets were also built around the town. Dustbins were neatly lined up outside each shop, which pleasantly gave way to filth free streets. People in general seemed happy, healthy and all the more helpful.

The Commissioner started to evaluate all that he was seeing, realising that there was some truth in what Shivlal had said. What the reason for this sea - change could possibly be, he had no idea as yet, but that there was a visible positive change in the look and feel of the town, was undeniable. All these things he saw were the signs of a **HAPPY TOWN WITH HAPPY RESIDENTS**, and through experience he knew that this in itself was a strong indicator of a low crime rate.

Commissioner Desai carried on strolling, and went down a by-lane where he knew the town hospital was situated. As he walked in, the first thing he noticed was the hospital walls, which were freshly painted. He walked towards the well maintained reception area and decided to get some more information about the improvements in the hospital, by donating some blood. A nurse who saw him waiting, went up to him with a pleasant smile, "How may I help you Sir? Sorry to keep you waiting. Pooja, our receptionist will be here in a while." The Commissioner was taken aback with the warm greeting - something that is not very common in small hospitals.

"I would like to donate some blood," said the Commissioner. "Oh! Thank you for being so kind and thoughtful! With God's grace, we have sufficient amount of blood available in our hospital's blood bank right now," replied the neatly dressed nurse humbly. This puzzled the Commissioner further, as blood in most Indian hospitals was always short in supply.

The Commissioner told the nurse that he was from another town and was visiting some friends in Gauraj Nagar. He further remarked that the hospital looked surprisingly fresh and clean. "Oh, thank you for the compliment!" said the nurse with a beaming smile on her face. "We now get a lot of volunteers on a regular basis that help us with the **up-keep** of the hospital. Townspeople also regularly come and devote their precious time, assisting us with taking basic care of patients. Some of them even got the paint themselves and painted the children's ward in bright colors."

"The number of common diseases such as stomach infections and influenza have also significantly gone down, thereby reducing our work

Proof of the Truth

load. We now have the time to focus only on patients that need extensive treatment." "When did all this begin?" questioned the Commissioner curiously, "I remember the last time I was here, all this did not exist!" "Oh, it's been almost over three months now," said the nurse, "We deeply and whole - heartedly thank our beloved bank branch manager, Mr. Atul Upadhay, for all this change. He has transformed Gauraj Nagar into a dream destination,without spending a single rupee!"

Commissioner Desai was perplexed and intrigued at the same time. "This is great, but how was Mr. Atul able to achieve this?" **he asked**, "What exactly did he do that changed the face of this town so drastically?" He recalled Shivlal mentioning the bank manager and some new scheme that he had apparently invented. Could it be the same thing? Just as the nurse was about to answer, a patient was wheeled in, and she ran off to assist him. "Ah, well," shrugged the Commissioner, and he slowly walked out of the hospital, still puzzled.

Commissioner Desai got back on to the streets to investigate further, and decided to stop for a quick bite somewhere. Upon finding a small eatery and devouring a plate of steaming hot dhoklas, he threw the paper plate in which he had eaten right where he was standing, out of habit. He was shaken out of his reverie by the stern voice of the eatery's owner, telling him to pick up the paper and drop it in the dustbin nearby. The vendor further added, "We are proud of our clean town and choose to maintain it. Please do not litter here!" Shame-faced, the Commissioner picked up the paper and dropped it in the dustbin nearby, and walked away.

> "You cannot force someone to comprehend a message that they are not ready to receive. Still, you must never underestimate the power of planting a seed"
> – Author Unknown

Finding another small restaurant a few hundred meters away from the previous one, the Commissioner walked in and sat down at an empty table. He noticed once again that even this restaurant bore a clean and cheerful atmosphere. By that time, he felt his imagination was surely painting this entire picture in front of him. "As policemen, we are supposed to be hard - hearted and deal with facts. We cannot and should not get carried away by all this 'good atmosphere' nonsense!" he told himself, sternly.

The positive vibe around was something that the Commissioner couldn't ignore. As all these thoughts ran through his mind, a waiter came up to him and greeted him warmly. The Commissioner wished him back and ordering a cup of tea, glanced around the restaurant. This place was clean and well maintained too. No vegetable peels lying around, the kitchen area was clean, no flies sitting on the tables, and everyone present there also looked hygienic.

By now, Commissioner Desai's amazement reached another level. "Damn!" he exclaimed, to himself, "What is all this that I'm seeing? This happens only in the big cities! A small town like Gauraj Nagar? I mean how on earth did this happen?"

Commissioner Desai stepped out of the little restaurant as quickly as possible, and went on to look out for something that he could complain about. As he walked on towards the end of the street from the restaurant, he heard a loud screech, followed by a thud. He immediately rushed towards the scene, where some men had already gathered. He saw there an injured Brahmin who had fallen off his bike, being helped by some Muslim men who had just finished their daily prayers at the mosque close by. It was heart-warming for the Commissioner to watch these men, who despite having cultural and communal differences were making an effort to help one another, especially in times of such emergencies.

The Commissioner by now was convinced that there was a turnaround in Gauraj Nagar, that too in a largely SPIRITUAL way. The change was undeniable and extremely positive, hence, he came to the conclusion to leave things as they were and not bother himself too much over it. He, like Shivlal Nayee, came from the school of thought which believed that one needs to investigate only if there is something negative that is happening. If there is any positive change, one should not rock the boat, but just be thankful and let sleeping dogs lie.

As it is, he had too much to do with the meager time instead of interfering when things were obviously going right. If there were any negative making his presence felt in Gauraj Nagar, the Commissioner returned to his headquarters in Keshav Nagar, that same night. A happily convinced, but unfortunately not a wiser man.

> "An intelligent person doesn't need the promise of heaven to see the merit in good deeds."
> – Unknown

08

Happÿness bank

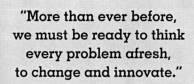

"More than ever before,
we must be ready to think
every problem afresh,
to change and innovate."

- J.R.D. Tata

Finding New Avenues

Forty - five - year - old Rohinton Talati was the heir of a vastly successful business family, which had built its corporate empire and reputation on the basis of rock solid and functional ethics. A young looking engineer and MBA graduate from the premier institutes of USA, Rohinton was a man who believed that employees and customers were the bedrock of any sound business. He was ever looking to expand his existing business empire, which already consisted of steel, automobiles, shipping, aviation, banking, and many more industries, into new uncharted areas where even his forefathers hadn't ventured so far. Being a man with both a mission and broad vision, he made a continuous effort to find new and better ways of leading, managing, and motivating his workforce.

Rohinton Talati's business empire was spread far and wide across the Indian sub-continent, apart from the Western side, the heartland of the country. He desired to set up a home-appliances manufacturing business to rival the Chinese and the Koreans. Home-appliances were a jewel yet missing in the crown of Talati Industries. Washing machines, air-conditioners, television sets, refrigerators, laptops - these were what had made organisations such as Samsung and LG into world-renowned names.

Rohinton was determined to make the name of Talati Industries renowned, not only in India, but all over the world. With this thought in mind, and with the guidance of some of his advisors, Rohinton Talati zeroed in on two or three districts in Western India, to set up a world-class home - appliance plant - Pingaleshwar being one of those shortlisted districts. As luck would have it, Commissioner Arvind Desai and Rohinton Talati turned out to be school friends. "Let us go down to Pingaleshwar District in Gujarat, first." said Talati, "Co-incidentally, the Commissioner in charge there is a good old friend of mine. He shall be able to guide us better on which town would be the most feasible for our project."

He envisioned a state of the art factory, and determined to put his best efforts in making this proposed project a success. Rohinton wanted to build something that everyone could associate Talati Industries with, instead of just their steel, automobiles and banking sectors. "This is my dream project, as you all are already aware. I don't want to take any more chances," concluded Talati cautiously.

A couple of years ago, Talati Industries had attempted to set up this factory in a Southern Indian state, on a piece of land that they had purchased legally. As soon as the construction began, trouble started to brew up. A local politician, with an eye on vote-bank politics, had aroused the local population into wrongly believing that Talati Industries would destroy the environment of the locality, and also their means of livelihood by converting their ancestral agricultural land into a vast desolate factory area. This, the politician proclaimed, would result in the loss of natural resources such as trees and water. The local population, gullible and easily influenced, succumbed to the wiles of this politician and held protests against Talati Industries.

The resistance to the factory reached such cataclysmic proportions, that Rohinton and his team were forced to withdraw from the state, with their plans for a grand factory destroyed by an individual who claimed to be a self - appointed Messiah of the down-trodden. Unfortunately, in reality the selfish eye was on an elected representative seat. Rohinton, being justifiably cautious, gave a call to his old friend Commissioner Desai and told him that he would like to meet him soon. An elated Commissioner Desai asked him to come over to the District Headquarters the following weekend.

> *"Good business leaders create a vision,*
> *articulate the vision, passionately own the vision,*
> *and relentlessly drive it to completion."*
> – Jack Welch

Rohinton Talati, accompanied by his two trusted advisors, Sumeet Dave and Rajesh Shah, reached Keshav Nagar by car from the domestic airport at Durjabad. Keshav Nagar was situated in the Pingaleshwar District

Finding New Avenues

and was also where the Police Headquarters of the district was situated. Commissioner Desai welcomed his old friend with gusto.

It was a matter of pride for the entire Pingaleshwar District that a renowned business personality was visiting them, with the stature of being the head of Talati Industries. Rohinton had not disclosed the reason of his official visit, since he wanted to seek advice and discuss about his project in person.

Three executive suites were booked at the best hotel in Keshav Nagar for the esteemed visitors. After resting for a while and freshening up, Rohinton invited the Commissioner over to the hotel for dinner. After exchanging pleasantries, Rohinton introduced his colleagues to the Commissioner and sat down at the table reserved for them. Commissioner Desai asked Rohinton Talati almost immediately after settling down, if there was a specific reason for this sudden visit. He intuitively knew that his friend surely had something on his mind. Else, a man like Rohinton Talati with his ultra - busy schedule, wouldn't have traveled all the way to Keshav Nagar, just to meet an old friend.

Rohinton Talati explained to Commissioner Desai in detail, everything about the dream project. Right from the reason he intended to build it, to the strengths and the challenges it had previously faced. "So you see, Arvind," said Rohinton, "Setting up the plant in a town which is relatively trouble - free, whose townspeople are willing to work hard and contribute to the company's success instead of hindering at every stage, is extremely imperative."

Commissioner Desai listened to each of his friend's words with utmost patience. "Hmm. I would quickly like to recapitulate in a nutshell what I have understood," said the Commissioner with his eyes shut, trying to visualize Rohinton's words, "Your dream project will manufacture world-class refrigerators, washing machines, televisions and other such household electronic equipment for the domestic as well as the export market. You are keen on setting up the factory in a peaceful locality, where you would get the support of the local population. Lastly, you had previously commenced this project in a state where the land you purchased, ran you into some unwanted political trouble."

"**Spot** on Arvind! That's perfectly summed up!" said Rohinton Talati with a broad smile, "You're still as sharp as you were, back in the school days. Marriage hasn't dulled your senses!" he joked, nudging Arvind Desai gently. "You are still as humorous, Rohinton. Anyway, coming back to your issue, I think I have half a solution to this," said the Commissioner. "Half a solution?" asked Rohinton, taken aback and unsure of what he had just heard, "What does half a solution mean Arvind?"

"**Well,**" responded the Commissioner, speaking slowly and choosing his words well, "What I meant is, I can only give you a partial suggestion. I am not sure of why and how it will work and benefit you, but maybe it shall work for you. I personally saw this in action recently, at a town nearby." "What on earth are you talking about, Arvind? Your riddling habit doesn't seem to have left you from the younger days!" said Rohinton, now a little irritated.

"**Patience,** my dear friend, patience," giggled the Commissioner, "I meant what I said. I only have half the solution to your dilemma. Let me explain. I can tell you where, but I can't tell you why. There is a town called Gauraj Nagar, a short drive **from Keshav Nagar**. The people there are exactly the type of people you are looking for - community oriented, motivated, hard-working, spiritually inclined, **united**, and **generally** happy. The mysterious thing is, they were not like that till just a few months ago. There has been a sudden transformation in them and their perspectives in life. The crime rate in that town, which was hovering around average before **an** earthquake had struck there, in today's date, is down to nil. It's great as far as I am concerned. If you wish to visit Gauraj Nagar, I can take you there tomorrow and introduce you to the town elders. You can take it forward from there, the way you want," concluded Commissioner Desai. "Well," said Rohinton, intrigued by his friend's explanation.

"**I** surely don't mind taking a look! Let us meet and leave early tomorrow morning then, gentlemen." In due course of time, the men gathered there all dispersed and retired for the night.

> "The fragrance of flowers spread only in the direction of the wind. But the goodness of a person spreads in all directions."
> – Chanakya

09

Happÿness
bank

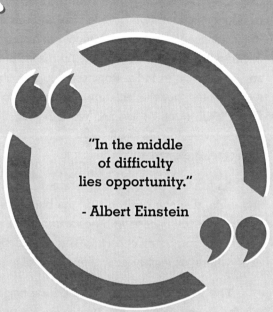

"In the middle
of difficulty
lies opportunity."

- Albert Einstein

Infinite
Possibilities

At 7 a.m. the next morning, Commissioner Desai, Rohinton Talati and his two advisors, set out on an official visit to Gauraj Nagar. The two-and-a-half-hour drive was traversed along the dusty highway, from the Keshav Nagar district headquarters to Gauraj Nagar, in two cars. As they entered the outskirts of Gauraj Nagar, Rohinton peeped out of the window to have an overview of the town. The buildings by themselves were by no means outstanding- replicas of almost any small town in India. Rohinton couldn't obviously immediately put his finger on the fact that this town appeared to be a HAPPIER and a more CHEERFUL place to live and work in. Yet, there was an undeniable and different vibe to this small town, just as they were entering. It definitely didn't feel like disaster had struck it.

As the MD of his conglomerate, Rohinton had obviously traveled far and wide, thus, he noticed that the building exteriors were brighter, the roads of the town were visibly cleaner and the simple townspeople seemed generally happy and cheerful. This was a sight that was not common everywhere, especially in smaller towns of India.

The vehicles halted outside Gauraj Nagar police station. Shivlal had left for Gauraj Nagar a day before, instructed to be ready to receive his boss and the distinguished guests. Ideally, the guests should have been directly taken to their hotel, but Commissioner Desai was eager to showcase a little bit of his domain as well. "A very good morning, Sirs," saluted a clean shaven and neatly dressed Shivlal Nayee, "A warm welcome to Gauraj Nagar. I hope you shall have a comfortable stay here. Everything has been arranged for, as per your taste and convenience. If you may need anything, kindly do not hesitate to let us know. We shall be at your service immediately." Shivlal had been made to parrot out this little speech, which he had practiced repeatedly since the previous evening.

The Commissioner smiled. This was the efficiency he liked to see from his subordinates, especially when he was in the presence of gentlemen with the stature of Rohinton Talati's. "Yes, good morning Shivlal," replied the Commissioner, stiffly yet as pleasantly as he could, "Kindly get us some mineral water quickly. We would like to visit the bank as soon as possible. I have spoken to the bank manager, Mr. Atul Upadhyay, yesterday. Mr. Talati here has a matter of great importance to be discussed with him. You did mention that Mr. Atul was partially responsible for the transformation, and the zero crime rate in Gauraj Nagar, didn't you?" he reconfirmed with Shivlal, a little anxiously. "Of course Sir, of course," answered Shivlal, "Though, without active support and co-operation from our local police force, nothing worthwhile can ever be accomplished!" he added, eager to share the limelight.

Rohinton could have easily invited Atul and the town elders over to his head office in Mumbai, and put them up in any of the best five-star hotels. He chose to meet Atul personally at the bank with a reason. Too often, Rohinton had been told tall tales by enthusiastic individuals, who were only eager to get some investments to rock their sunken boats. Hence, he wanted to inspect things first - hand, and not rely on information from secondary sources, however trusted they might be. Rohinton wasn't willing to invest in the town until he was thoroughly convinced that the local populace was willing and eager to participate in the shared fruits of prosperity, this factory would bring.

Atul brought Rohinton out of his reverie as soon as they reached the bank. "Good morning, respected Sirs," he greeted them warmly, "It is an honour for Gauraj Nagar and our bank, to have you and your colleagues

visit us. I hope whatever it is that you are looking for, you will be able to find here." Rohinton beamed with pleasure. He immediately took a liking to this soft-spoken man, who on one hand looked so ordinary, and on another, generated a feeling of implicit trust. He also noticed and appreciated the fact that Atul greeted his colleagues as well, with equal amount of respect. On most occasions, due to Rohinton's larger than life image, people often forget to show their respects to his subordinates, who are men of repute and standing too. Rohinton's respect for Atul immediately soared as he noted this gesture.

Atul led the guests to his cabin, where chairs befitting the status of the visitors had been arranged at short notice. A few town elders such as the school principal and the head of municipality were already present there, awaiting the dignitaries. The occasion was indeed overwhelming for the town, similar to what would have been the occasion if the Pope from Rome was to visit the local church at Gauraj Nagar. Once introductions and formal greetings had been exchanged, Rohinton got straight to the point and explained to everyone present in detail, the reason for his visit.

Atul and the town elders attentively listened to every word Rohinton Talati spoke. As soon as Rohinton finished explaining, Atul in his usual humble manner, summarised all that he had understood, "Sir, I thank you for the confidence you have evinced in the people of our small town. I also thank Commissioner Desai for recommending us to you. As you might already be aware, our town has recently seen a radical change for the better. The zero crime rates that you have heard of are merely one of the effects. The people of Gauraj Nagar have put in a lot of effort to be happy and healthy in general. They have transformed this town, making it a pleasure to live in. Credit for this improvement goes to every single person in Gauraj Nagar."

"I truly believe, Sir, that every individual is inherently good. No one is born as a bad person. After all, as our scriptures say, we are embodiments of the Creator Himself. We allow the force of circumstances to take over us as we grow. We may temporarily lose our way, but all that is needed at such times is a **RAY OF LIGHT**. This town went through a terrible natural calamity, during the course of which each one of us suffered beyond description. All we did was, got together as a team, and came up with a little idea which we believed was our ray of light. This not only helped us get over our depression but also helped us grow into better individuals," concluded Atul.

> "There are no business problems,
> management problems, leadership problems,
> or profit problems. There are only people problems."
> – Dan Waldschmidt

Rohinton Talati, his advisors and the Commissioner were all stunned at how simply Atul had explained the visibly humongous change in Gauraj Nagar. "Well," said the school principal, seeing that Atul was in no mood to highlight his own brainwave, "Apologies for interrupting, but, I must. On the hundredth day after the earthquake, the entire town gathered to hear a couple of us speak.

We only wanted to motivate these simple townspeople, and help them to find a way to mentally rise above their depression. Mr. Atul here, who is a spiritually inclined gentleman, quoted to us from religious scriptures of almost every faith. We were reminded of the eternal truth - *happiness and change comes from within and begins with us*. The principal further added, "Most of us know all this, only to realise we were only passively listening to what the religious heads kept propagating. We never put what we knew and had learned into action, maybe because we didn't have any guidelines to practice what was being preached."

> "Love alone confers lasting happiness and peace.
> Sharing can alone reduce grief and multiply joy.
> People are born to share, to serve, to give and not to grab."
> – Sathya Sai Baba

The principal then spoke about the **Bank of Good Karma** and the **Good Deed Passbook** which Atul had conceived, and the town elders had fine-tuned. "How does a tiny passbook, that only **RECOGNISES** and

Infinite Possibilities

RECORDS good deeds, motivate people to do so much good and change their outlook on everything? I mean, without expectation of any reward, the entire town has gone through a sea of positive change. How?" asked a stunned Rohinton Talati.

"That is indeed the beauty of it," replied the principal, "People do like to do good for others, if they can be convinced that by doing so, they shall be benefitted in the long run. Of course, we would have surely liked to give them some sort of a physical **REWARD** along with **RECOGNITION** of the good deeds, but we don't have the resources to do that, as of now. Anyway, even without the reward angle, the idea seems to have served its purpose. People are now **HABITUATED** to doing good things and that is all that matters. A psychological research has proven that, if one does an activity continuously for twenty-one days, that activity becomes a habit. This is exactly what has happened. Doing good and being good is now a **HABIT** in Gauraj Nagar."

Rohinton was completely blown away by everything he had just heard. "What if," he thought, having a eureka moment just like Atul did during his speech, "We carry this idea forward on a larger scale, and not only **RECORD** and **RECOGNISE** the **GOOD DEEDS**, but also **REWARD** them? After all, our organisation has the resources and capability to provide a decent reward along with the record and the recognition."

Before committing to anything, even verbally, he first had to clarify, "It sounds very nice, but are you sure there is no other reason for this change you have witnessed in Gauraj Nagar?" asked Rohinton, "Any other factor which might be responsible for this sudden improvement? Is it really only due to this passbook of a hypothetical **'BANK OF GOOD KARMA'**, which you feel has done the trick? I mean, I would want to believe it and I also do feel deep within that it's possible, but it's such a simple solution! It sounds so basic. That is what is still making me hesitate to believe in it as a **'MIRACLE CURE!'"**

Atul replied to this question with a smile, "Yes Sir. It precisely works because it is simple and basic. Human beings are deep within, simple beings wrapped up in an external cloak of complexity. We often fail to tap into the potential hidden within a person, simply because we try complex routes to reach his mind. History has often proven, that what works to get people to do and be their best, is achieved through their heart, not their minds alone."

"**Do** not all religions and their scriptures teach us things in the simplest of ways? Is there any religious book that one would find difficult to comprehend? God has made this world a beautiful and simple place. We have complicated, and at many times misused what we have been given. God gave us trees, we made axes out of them. God gave us minerals to use for good purposes, it is us who used them in guns and cannons. God also gave us sweet fruits and juicy vegetables to live a happy and healthy life. Once again, it is us who made chemically refined products out of them and poisoned our bodies. Sir, I say this with all my heart - *nothing is as powerful as a simple idea with noble intent, well executed*. Have faith, Sir, have faith. God is in His Heaven and all will be right with this world."

> "If an egg is broken by an outside force, life ends.
> If an egg is broken by a force from inside, then life begins.
> Great things only happen from the inside."
> – Unknown

As Atul concluded his heart-felt explanation, the school principal and the head of the municipality, stared at him - awe-struck by his eloquence. They had heard Atul speak before, but that was always at local gatherings or amongst known people. Here, Atul was addressing one of the most powerful industrialists in India, that too with confidence and conviction.

All eyes turned to Rohinton, to gauge his reaction. Just then, he serenely smiled and got up from his chair, with an applause, "I'm bought!" he exclaimed, with visibly damp eyes, "In fact, I would want to improvise this further. As Isaac Newton got his brainwave when he sat below the apple tree and an apple fell on him - he discovered the Law of Gravity, similarly Mr. Atul, your words and your idea have struck a chord in me which I believe, can **REVOLUTIONIZE CORPORATE FUNCTIONING!**"

Rohinton quickly closed his laptop, getting ready to leave, "If you don't mind, gentlemen, could we please conclude this meeting here? I would like some time alone by myself and chisel what I've thought of. Could we all please meet in our hotel lobby in a few hours to take this forward? As much as I am making no promises now, I somehow feel we have found the perfect site for my dream factory project." "Sure," said Atul, a little unsure what had just happened since the meeting ended abruptly.

> "The best way to find yourself,
> is to lose yourself in the service of others."
> – Mahatma Gandhi

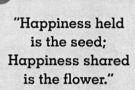

"Happiness held
is the seed;
Happiness shared
is the flower."

– John Harrigan

An Idea that moved Mountains

Rohinton met Atul and the town elders later that evening at the hotel's coffee shop. Rohinton once again got straight to the point without wasting much time, "I have been thinking," he began, "And the more I thought, the more sense your words made. I also took a stroll near the hotel and saw for myself; all that you and Commissioner Desai had mentioned about the place and people. This town is definitely much cleaner, and the people are much happier than in similar towns across the country. There is a unique VIBE around this place, which is positively infectious. If as you say, this is because of the passbook scheme you have introduced, and which the townspeople have been the happy beneficiaries of, I would like to carry your brilliant idea on to the next level."

"I now intend, with your assistance of course, to identify a suitable plot of land nearby, large enough for setting up our factory. My legal team, architects and civil engineers shall be involved at a later stage. For any initiative to succeed, the human resource factor is of utmost importance. So, while you Mr. Atul, and the town elders, with certain financial limitations have succeeded merely by **RECOGNISING** and **RECORDING GOOD DEEDS** in a passbook, I feel the same scheme can take off at a larger level and work more effectively, if we introduce a **THIRD 'R'** into it - **THE REWARD**. Our business group has the resources to provide these rewards."

"Let me be honest, if you think in offering **REWARDS** for the **GOOD DEEDS,** I and my organisation are being selfish, then yes, we are. But this is surely in a positive and healthy way. Every relationship that exists on this material plane of ours, has an element of expectation attached with it. For example, if a boss pays an employee a salary, he expects work in return. If a friend attends your family wedding, he does expect that you will also attend his function in the future. Giving and receiving is the oil that smoothens all human relationships and keeps them on track. Thus, it becomes a **WIN-WIN** situation for all."

"To begin with, I would first like to have a look at the **GOOD DEED PASSBOOK** that you provided the townspeople. Simultaneously, I shall have my strategising team come up with a detailed list of staffing and other requirements in terms of skill-sets needed from the workforce. We can then make a Good Deed List, similar to the one you have made, and chalk out the **POINT** and **REWARD** structure.

"**If** I may add further, I am keen on **IMPLEMENTING** this concept across all organisations within our conglomerate and not just this proposed factory. As for all you wonderful gentlemen here, I assure you that you shall get due credit for conceptualising the **GOOD DEED BANK.** I shall do everything I can and make this work."

"**I** am most impressed by the comprehensive **GOOD DEED LIST** you have compiled, Mr. Atul. It is absolutely keeping in mind with the need of the hour for a town of Gauraj Nagar's size. Anyway, I guess I should end this meeting here. I shall return in a few days after having a discussion with my core team members and directors, back at our headquarters."

"**I** truly hope to see this as the start of a beautiful relationship between Gauraj Nagar and Talati Industries. Thank you for all the warmth and hospitality. It truly has been an enlightening experience visiting this town, and all you wonderful souls. God Bless!" Rohinton had finally found what he was looking for, and the people of Gauraj Nagar had been blessed even more, with yet another wonderful opportunity to change and better their lives further.

> "Do your little bit of good wherever you are.
> It's those little bits of good
> put together that overwhelm the world."
> – Desmond Tutu

Happÿness
bank

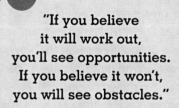

"If you believe
it will work out,
you'll see opportunities.
If you believe it won't,
you will see obstacles."

– Wayne Dyer

Goodness
with a
Corporate twist

Dr. Balakrishna, Head of Human Resources at one of the Talati Companies, was a firm believer in the power of people. Rohinton upon his arrival back in Mumbai, discussed Gauraj Nagar and the successful exercise Atul had conducted with his BANK OF GOOD KARMA, at length with him. Dr. Balakrishna was one of the senior most employees of Talati Industries, having an experience of over twenty - five years of dealing with all kinds of people, right from the factory workers to the CEOs.

Rohinton elaborated on how he intended to take Atul's scheme forward on a larger scale. "This shall revolutionize the function of Human Resources," Dr. Balakrishna said, also expressing his views about the corporate world, "For way too long, we have been talking about Human Resources as being a strategic partner in business, but, we haven't witnessed anything concrete till date. I am keen on seeing a revolutionary idea emerge, such as this you have just mentioned, which could change the face of Human Resource Management in itself."

"Around five-hundred years ago, the field of finance witnessed the introduction of the *double-entry system of accounts*. We then had to wait for another five hundred years for the next big idea - *the triple bottom line*, which ensures that businesses do not just focus on profitability but also on the planet and its people. This and the emergence of Environmental Concerns and Corporate Social Responsibility, have changed the way in which Corporate Houses are viewed today. Similarly Rohinton, I have faith after listening to you, that this concept, though at a nascent stage, has the potential to be the biggest motivational force of the twenty-first century - indeed, the greatest motivating power in all of history!"

Rohinton Talati had a broad smile on his face. Dr. Bala, as he was popularly known in the company, was a pretty conservative man. He was always a little sceptical and cautious towards any new concept that was introduced in the company. Rohinton felt that if this concept of the **BANK OF GOOD KARMA** could get Dr. Bala so excited and charged up, the idea was definitely meritorious!

"Let's have an early morning meeting organised with our think-tank, Dr. Bala. Please ask everyone to postpone their work and meetings. I'm informing my secretary to reschedule all my appointments too.

What I have in mind, which as you rightly said, is going to make this the biggest Human Resource innovation, that not only our industry and country, but probably our entire planet has ever witnessed!" a beaming Rohinton said, excited to announce the scheme to everyone."

> *"As we look ahead into the next century, leaders will be those who empower others."*
> – Bill Gates

At precisely 9 a.m. the next morning, some of the top executives of the conglomerate and the finest brains in the country, gathered into the boardroom. "Ladies and gentlemen," began Rohinton, "I am sorry to disturb your schedule, that too at such a short notice, but the agenda of this meeting itself is such." "Don't worry," he smiled, as he saw their grim faces, "There is no bad news. Actually, this makes me wonder. Why is it that when we hear of some urgency, it is always assumed to be a problem, or something negative? Our brains seem to have been hard-wired over the years, to assume that if we are called out urgently, there must be something wrong. We give all our energy and focus to that. Unfortunately, the media has not been helpful either. Good news does not make that big a headline as much as a disaster does. Please do take a moment and contemplate. An urgency can also be something positive. Maybe someone has good news to give you. Well, ladies and gentlemen, without further ado, let me get to the reason why I have gathered you all here."

Rohinton, thereafter, narrated everything about Atul, Gauraj Nagar, the **BANK OF GOOD KARMA** with the **GOOD DEED PASSBOOK**, and how this idea fitted in with the search for their new factory's location. "We have surely solved the issue of finding the most apt location for this new factory. "But," he paused, as a roaring applause followed the announcement, "This is just one of the reasons for which we are gathered here today.

"In all the factories we have set up till date, we have always fallen behind schedule, and usually have been above the allocated budget. The fault has not been in our projections. They have always been made with

Goodness with a Corporate twist

great care, by all you experienced people. The problem has largely been due to the lack of trained, motivated and committed people that work at the factories.

Let us be honest, you and I are sitting here because there are people working at the factories. We are all connected to each other like a chain. If those people that actually make our products are not motivated enough to give their hundred percent, how can we as managers, function at our optimum level?

"The fault does not lie with the people alone. It also lies in our existing system. The current way in which we manage everything, right from recruitment, selection and training, to our employee engagement and motivational strategies is all wrong. Our system does not truly consider people as individuals, with unique needs and aspirations of their own. We always look at keeping the interests of our organisation foremost, which is not a bad thing, but sometimes, in doing so, we tend to alienate the individuals who work for us. If we are the car, those workers are the wheels of the car that make it run on the roads. In this context, our employees should have the feeling of working with us and not really for us. Only then, can we work and achieve maximum success as a team."

"I honestly went to Gauraj Nagar with little but HOPE, and have returned with CONVICTION that not only have we found the right place, but also identified a unique system that can lead us to SUCCESS BORN FROM SYNERGY. I have gathered you all here today to share and explain the idea that I have been introduced to. With your valuable feedback, we can fine-tune and implement it throughout our organisation. This idea should be extrapolated across all our various businesses. Old and new; factories and offices; for workers, supervisors and managers; in small towns and in metro cities. It is not limited to getting our new factory made up and running in some kind of record time," said Rohinton, deciding to pause for a while, take a breath and let all that he had said, be imbibed by those present."

> "Management is about arranging and telling. Leadership is about nurturing and enhancing."
> – Tom Peters

The assembled audience wore mixed expressions on their faces. The optimists seemed as excited as Rohinton. These were the people, who were always interested in new ideas and believed in change. Then there were the cynical-minded, who looked sceptical as always.

They thought they had seen too many fads come and go to generate enthusiasm for any new idea, before they actually heard it out, evaluated it, and studied its pros and cons. Rohinton, though relatively young, had mastered various behavioral patterns and chose his next words with great care, ensuring he struck the right chord with everyone.

Rohinton was sure that these individuals in front of him would be instrumental in ensuring the success of the proposed concept in the organisation, once it was approved and implemented. "The general perception in business is," he continued, "When one wins, the other loses. The beauty of this concept lies in the fact that, it is a **WIN-WIN** concept. Everybody wins here - the organisation, management, employees, customers, and the society at large. The **GOOD DEED PASSBOOK** and its implementation, transformed Gauraj Nagar, a tragedy-stricken small town, into an oasis of positivity and goodness. This passbook simply **RECORDED** and **RECOGNISED GOOD DEEDS** that the townspeople did, the eligibility of which was decided by a small council, consisting of certain townspeople. The **GOOD DEED PASSBOOK** has led to such an addictive **FEEL GOOD FACTOR,** that the people of Gauraj Nagar are habituated mentally to do and feel good. They are in a constant **DO-GOOD MODE.**

"We can also introduce such a system for all our employees at Talati Industries in a professional manner, not only by **RECOGNIZING** and **RECORDING** the good work they do, but also **REWARDING** them for it. Trust me. The **POSITIVE ENERGY** we can generate from this will be unimaginable. Our ancient wisdom tells us, and modern science confirms - *our Universe is made of matter and energy.* By **REWARDING** the **GOOD DEEDS**, we can convert the latent energy that lies within people into action. The **REWARDS** will ensure that the direction in which this latent energy is channelised will be **UPLIFTING**, and the materialistic results will benefit all concerned. These rewards will simply act as a catalyst."

Goodness with a Corporate twist

The look on the faces of most of the people gathered in the conference room was getting animated. Not to deny that Rohinton's energy and drive was raising their enthusiasm, to a totally different level. The Financial Controller of the organisation pointed out, "Are we not already paying enough to our employees? We are already appraising their performance, and giving them regular incentives and promotions for the good job they do. Are you suggesting that we reward them even more for simply doing their duty?"

Rohinton smiled. This was just the question he had been waiting for so he could add the thrust and twist to the concept he had seen and had refined in his fertile mind. "Thank you so much for bringing up this vital point," Rohinton replied, "This has brought me to the crux of the matter. The **GOOD DEEDS** we propose to **RECOGNISE**, **RECORD**

and **REWARD,** will have nothing to do with the work the employees have already been selected for and are being paid to do. We shall **REWARD** them for **DOING GOOD TO SOCIETY** - good deeds similar to those the townspeople of Gauraj Nagar I have just told you about."

"But Sir," the Financial Controller argued further, "If we are going to make them do good things for the society, then when will they get time to do their jobs?" "The townspeople of Gauraj Nagar also have jobs to do," Rohinton replied, almost sarcastically, "Their contribution to society is done in some part of their spare time, and they are doing all this without even being rewarded for the same. Look, I do not propose that our employees put in long hours doing these good deeds.

We will prepare our list of **GOOD DEEDS** that our entire organization can participate in, and structure an appropriate **REWARD SYSTEM** for the same. We will factor in a wide range of activities into this list, and our employees can choose areas which match their interests, skill sets and suit their convenience best. Participation for this will be on a purely on a voluntary basis."

"I have already shown you all a sample of the list which Mr. Atul, the bank manager of Gauraj Nagar, has formulated for his townspeople. With our qualified people to work on the same, we can definitely come out with a more comprehensive list. We can then add the **ELEMENT OF REWARD** to it, which is missing in the Gauraj Nagar list."

"Society now expects corporate houses to contribute to its **UPLIFTMENT** - and this is only right, since we utilise scarce resources of the society. We have to return back to the world, what we take, beyond the normal materialistic giving and taking. Not only is this the right thing to do, but research has shown that corporate houses which participate in such societal activity, also gain huge **POSITIVE GOODWILL,** which is impossible to attain through any amount of creative advertising alone.

"Today over fifty percent of the assets column on the balance sheets of many leading brands, is made up of the component of goodwill. Umpteen number of organisations undertake some sort of societal activity. In fact, as of 2014, the Indian government has made the contribution of organisations towards Social Responsibility compulsory, even insisting that 2 percent of organisational profits be contributed towards the same. This is something all organisations will now have to do, mandatorily."

> "Management is about human beings. Its task is to make people capable of joint performance – to make their strengths effective, and their weakness irrelevant."
> – Peter Drucker

"So," Rohinton continued, "I know what is playing on your minds - how and why is this particular idea going to be different and path-breaking? The answer is very simple. I have conceptualised a formula based on the fact that, rather than randomly donating at different places from a management level, we shall involve all our employees in this process.

Each employee shall be encouraged to contribute towards uplifting society, in areas which he feels strongest about, and in ways he knows best. Furthermore, we shall **RECOGNISE** and **RECORD** the effort, eventually **REWARDING** them for the same."

"Trust me when I say this, every human being, has inherent within themselves, the passion and power to do good things. Unfortunately, passion in itself is not sufficient. This passion needs to be channelized in the right direction, with the right guidance, and should be backed by concrete action. People should be able and willing to give a little bit of their time and energy. In other words, this willingness of giving should come from their hearts. That is the only way this can succeed."

"You all know about the mathematical term PI, right?" questioned Rohinton, "The uniqueness of PI is that it is an infinite number - there is no known end to the numerals to which it can be calculated. Similarly, in the formula I have devised, we take P, the **PASSION** of an individual and multiply it by I, **INCENTIVIZING** the Passion, by adding points in the person's passbook. The points shall be entered in the **GOOD DEED PASSBOOK**, each time an employee performs a good deed. These points can then be added and eventually rewarded by tangible benefits. Everyone wins, infinitely," explained Rohinton, illustrating this formula in his own way, on a white-board.

"**Let** me give you a simple example," Rohinton said, noticing that some people still seemed a little lost with his explanation, "If you tell a child to do something good, repeatedly, do you think he would still do it? Maybe. But promise the child a sweet in return for what he does, and see the light shine in his eyes. Notice how willing he would be to do what he is told to. In short, it is basic human psychology to work or do something passionately, if we know we are being rewarded for it in return in some way.

"**Hence,** in context with our proposed project, all we have to do is merely **HARNESS** the existing passion in an employee by incentivizing it in a structured manner, so that efforts and energy are channelized in the right direction. As an additional result, something good and worthwhile shall be done for the society as well. This honestly costs us nothing. We invest crores in all kinds of advertisements. Instead of that, why can't we invest lakhs in people for a change, encouraging them to do something good not only for themselves but for society as well? In doing this, not only shall we get some better trained and skilled staff for our organization, but it shall surely garner equal amount of publicity for us in a good and respectable manner.

"**The** result of this mutually beneficial exercise will be a Positively Profitable People - oriented Public - Private Partnership."

"**Any** questions till here?" asked Rohinton quickly, before moving ahead and getting to the main point, "Let us now get back to what should be our first step in this new activity. As a trial run, we shall first begin with the simple passbook method, similar to what Mr. Atul had come up with, that too, only with our staff at the upcoming factory. We shall later elaborate the process and build the reward system and implement it across our entire organisation."

"**Post** lunch, let us brainstorm and generate a list of **GOOD DEEDS** on the lines of Mr. Atul's list. This shall be a list of **GOOD DEEDS** that we can **RECOGNISE, RECORD** and **REWARD**. Please remember, this list should lead to a **WIN-WIN** situation. Also, before the list is created, kindly keep certain important points in mind before we start recruiting people for the new factory, such as -

- We need skilled and trained workforce at the factory.
- We need to ensure that these people are committed to work.
- The entire working population at the factory should be constantly motivated, to ensure wholehearted contribution, leading to the success of our proposed project.
- A sense of loyalty should be present in order to avoid any external influences to brain-wash the employees.

These are some of the issues we faced last time around. This is just precautionary so we don't run into any complication and waste more time. I am very sure, with this concept, we shall have established a **BOND** of **LOYALTY** and **LOVE** with our people. I have a lot of faith in this tiny little **GOOD DEED PASSBOOK**, since I have seen the proof of its implementation with my own eyes, in Gauraj Nagar. I truly believe that, *what gets* **RECOGNISED**, **RECORDED** *and* **REWARDED**, *shall be accomplished with enthusiasm, alacrity and gusto!*" Thus saying, Rohinton ended the first half of the meeting. Just like Atul, he too felt like he had been somewhat divinely blessed to speak whatever he did in the last few hours. As accomplished as he was academically and financially, this new factory seemed to give him a different perspective on life and success in general.

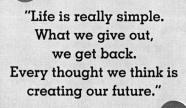

"Life is really simple.
What we give out,
we get back.
Every thought we think is
creating our future."

– Louise Hay

The Reward System

Rohinton's team produced a draft of the corporate **GOOD DEED LIST** on returning back into the conference room post-lunch. The first half of the list was to aid in setting up the new factory, and the other half extended to all the organisations within Talati Industries. For example, the employees were encouraged to travel either by a bicycle, car-pool or public transport to and from work, eliminate the usage of polythene bags, use a mobile handset for a minimum of two years, donate blood and organize blood donation drives, tutor under-privileged children, plant trees and look after them for at least six months.

Once the list was finalised and approved by the executives present, practical plans were made for its implementation. Initially at the Gauraj Nagar factory, and gradually throughout all the organisations of Talati Industries. The objective of the **BANK OF GOOD KARMA** and the **GOOD DEED PASSBOOK** was primarily two folds. Firstly, to get some of the locals rapidly trained in necessary skill-sets such as machine operating, carpentry, electrical-work, and so on. Secondly, every employee, whether a manager or a laborer at the factory, should be able to feel a sense of oneness with Talati Industries. This would strengthen not only bonds amongst each other but also ensure that any vested interests would not be able to alienate the townspeople against the organisation.

Rohinton Talati and his team estimated that setting up a state-of-the-art factory would ordinarily take around three and a half to four years. However, Rohinton was convinced that with the newly proposed scheme, the set-up time would easily be reduced by one year. This would not only save the company crores of rupees, but also benefit the workers and townspeople of Gauraj Nagar.

> *"Corporate strategy is usually only useful if you get people engaged with helping you to make it work."*
> – Max Mckeown

The usual problems associated with initiating a new project were more than known to Rohinton, some of them being unavailability of skilled labourers, resistance from local people to sell their land for the factory, existing employees of the company not willing to relocate to a small town and, local politicians instigating the town inhabitants to rebel against the setting up the factories, thereby extorting money from the industrialists.

To ensure no uneasy situations arise, Rohinton made sure he appointed the right managers for the factory and clearly chalked out what he wanted -

- Continuous Supply of skilled and committed laborers and supervisors.
- Constant upgradation of skills of the employees.
- A healthy working environment for the employees and the townspeople alike. The success of the factory would depend on the support of the locals, and their success in return, would depend on the success of the factory.
- Maintenance of hygiene in Gauraj Nagar and promoting health and fitness further. This would reduce absenteeism from work, thus increasing productivity.

To ensure the scheme that originated in Gauraj Nagar was translated professionally from where it had commenced, Rohinton and his team worked hard on creating two important lists that formed the crux of the scheme for the new factory. **LIST ONE** consisted of the possible **GOOD DEEDS,** and the points employees could receive for them. Once these points were accumulated to a certain amount, Talati Industries would give the **REWARDS** in terms of salary bonuses.

LIST TWO was drawn up for **GOOD DEEDS** that could be performed by the townspeople of Gauraj Nagar and a few neighboring towns. This list pertained to people who were not currently employed with Talati Industries. Since they were not entitled to get a salary or bonus, a special **REWARD** system was chalked out for them. (A sample of these two extensive lists and their rewards have been tabulated at the end of this book as appendix one)

The Reward System

The two lists put together would create a WIN-WIN situation for all concerned -

- Talati Industries would benefit since the factory would be up and running in record time, thereby saving crores of rupees.
- The employees would be benefited, as they would receive salary bonuses as rewards.
- The townspeople and the villagers would get free skill training. This would make an unskilled, illiterate townsperson, an asset to society - ensuring the prosperity of his family and thus, the entire town.
- The factory would get the support of the local population, which would create a harmonious work environment, and would do away with strikes and lock-outs.
- The factory would also get a continuous supply of skilled personnel, which would further save crores of rupees in recruitment and training activities.
- There would be a massive increase in an individual's self-worth, which would keep one motivated to work harder and better.

The locality would benefit in various ways as well -

- **Education** - Bigger and better schools would be built, which would increase the literacy and education rate.
- **Medical Care** - A bigger and a better hospital was planned, which would ensure better health and fitness for everyone.
- **Environment** - With better hygienic conditions, the environment would become cleaner, which would also result in better health.
- **Infrastructure** - Improved facilities of road, electricity, water and houses.
- **Security** - There would be sharp decrease in crime rate.
- **Prosperity** - There would be an increase in disposable income.
- **Happiness** - There would be a visible increase in the **HAPPINESS INDEX** of the entire locality.

> "If everyone is moving forward together,
> then success takes care of itself."
> – Henry Ford

Rohinton Talati and his team, after days of fine tuning, eventually implemented the **GOOD DEED** scheme at the upcoming factory in Gauraj Nagar. As expected, what they felt would be a trial run and could have a small possibility of failure, turned out to be a super phenomenal success instead. Rohinton's happiness knew no bounds and thus, without any further delay, he decided to immediately make plans and implement this scheme on a larger and better scale, across the entire Talati conglomerate. The **GOOD DEED PASSBOOK** would be given and used by every employee working with the Talati group of companies - right from the peons to the CEOs.

BANK of GOOD KARMA

.. a Talati Industries CSR Initiative

RECOGNISE
RECORD
REWARD

Account No. BGK - 205132

Employee Name: Anosh Batliwala

Employee Id: TI-358   **Department:** TI-358

Email: **Blood Group:** O+ve

Date	Activity	Points	Signature
14/5	Donated his old laptop worth 10,000.	2	
17/6	Provided six months training in sales to 3 semi skilled persons.	15	
20/9	Sponsored the education of a girl child from the locality.	5	

ÿ

Happÿness
bank

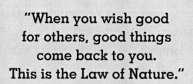

"When you wish good
for others, good things
come back to you.
This is the Law of Nature."

- Unknown

Ripple effects
of Giving

The aim of implementing the **GOOD DEED PASSBOOK** within the existing organisations of Talati Industries was slightly different. The intention here was, strengthening relationships amongst employees, which would strengthen societal acceptance of Talati Industries as a caring and socially responsible organisation. Additionally, there would be a steady supply of trained manpower at every level, within all the companies of Talati Industries.

Under the Corporate Social Responsibility department, which became an important part of Talati Industries, a sub-department was created which could technically take requests for help and assistance of different types from any citizen, NGOs, or organisations - including the less economically privileged employees of Talati industries. Every branch of the company offices or factory sites would have a representative from this department.

Rohinton improvised the scheme further in such a way, that any citizen of India could approach the nearest location of Talati Industries, and register their requirements with the CSR department there. For example, a person could register a requirement for a laptop or a mobile phone, while others could come with a requirement **of** books, furniture, etc. Some could come with the requirement of wanting funds for higher or even basic education, whereas some could have the requirement of wanting to learn and practice working on a lathe machine, or master the skill of **accounting.**

The requests were segregated into five categories-

Category 1: Monetary help - Employees could win points by providing monetary help to those under privileged, who had registered themselves under the CSR programs. The financial aid could be could be in areas of education, medical and surgery or skill-training.

Category 2: Non-monetary help in terms of used goods - Employees could win points by donating their used items such as laptops, computers, mobile phones, books, furniture, etc., to those who genuinely need them.

Category 3: Free skill training - Employees could win points providing free training to those unskilled people, who registered themselves with the CSR department.

Category 4: Providing free professional services - Employees could win points by providing free professional services such as filing tax returns, preparing accounts, handling legal paper work, etc., especially to those who were illiterate and elderly.

Category 5: Activities for environment and self-improvement - Employees could win points by participating in activities such as planting tree saplings, organizing cleanliness drives, using less paper, traveling by car pools, aiding someone less privileged, etc.

The requirements, after having their credibility checked, would be listed in the internal database of the **organisations'** website. Any employee of Talati Industries could access it and contribute for the same. For example, if there was a request for a mobile phone in Category 2 and a manager employed with Talati Industries wanted to discard his old phone for a new one, he could now rather than getting a paltry sum in exchange for it, give it away to someone who **would** genuinely make use of the phone. Simultaneously, this employee would be allotted a certain number of points in his passbook, for the **GOOD DEED he has** done.

> "Giving is not just about making a donation.
> It is about making a difference."
> – Kathy Calvin

This scheme benefitted everyone who chose to be a part of it. Whether it was a person who registered a requirement, or an individual who provided for the need. As thousands of employees also started using public transport or arranged car-pools, it noticeably saved a substantial amount of money, saved fuel and also reduced pollution. Less paper was also used and more trees were planted instead. Various schemes were floated continuously by the company, with attractive rewards, including promotions, additional monetary benefits in the form of insurance and home and car loans, etc.

Ripple effects of Giving

Talati Industries constructed a **GOOD DEED and REWARD TABLE**, across all the five categories:

Category 1 - Monetary help

Description	Points
Donating money to those in need, for a specified purpose	1 point for every Rs.1000 donated.

Category 2 - Non Monetary help in terms of used goods

Description	Points
Donating used items such as laptops, computers, mobiles, furniture, books, etc.	1 point for every Rs.1000, of every used item donated. (calculated on the used item's market value)

Category 3 - Free Skill Training

Description	Points
Providing free skill training.	5 points for every person successfully trained in a skill.

Category 4 - Providing free professional services.

Description	Points
Providing free professional services (taxation, legal, medical, etc.)	5 points for professional services provided to every person.

Category 5 - Activities for self and environmental improvement

Description	Points
Commuting via car pool or public transport at least twice a week. (for people travelling regularly by car)	1 point per week.
Using less than 100 printout sheets in their personal office per month	5 points per month.
Enrolling for substance de - addiction programs.	5 points per program.
Maintaining one's body weight.	1 point per month.
Enrolling for self - improvement courses within the company in the areas of marketing, accounts, soft-skills or leadership programs.	5 points per successful completion of each program.

> "Individual efforts can bring excellence,
> but only collective efforts can deliver effectively."
> – Narendra Modi

This entire process not only benefited Talati Industries by creating a strong bond amongst the employees, but also increased the sales of its products and services. This further resulted in a stronger brand equity and recall. The company was thus, able to connect with millions of people across the geography of the country, in a meaningful and mutually beneficial way.

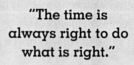

"The time is
always right to do
what is right."

- Martin Luther King Jr.

A
Paradigm
Shift

It began with little murmurs at the stock market. The little murmurs became loud whispers, and these loud whispers eventually became shouts. All of them said only one thing - there is something unusual happening at Talati Industries, which is zooming their profit graphs and rocketing them through the roof.

Well, profits are all that the investors and dealers of the stock markets are interested in, and rightly so. Higher profits don't materialise from thin air. They are accrued on a concrete commercial basis and a foundation of **HOPE**, that there are greater profits yet to come. This **HOPE** arises based on a keen observation of weekly, monthly and quarterly statements, which show the figures in rupees. This then decides whether the demand for the organization's shares will go north or south.

The Talati Group of Companies in the last six months, had become the toast of the Sensex. The analysts tried all they could to see exactly what it was that Talati Industries was doing differently. In an age of corporate espionage, where one organization could hardly breathe without its competitors knowing how much oxygen went into the lungs, it seemed amazing to these analysts that they had not identified any factor in six months, which could account for Talati Industries' healthy profits. No new technology had been developed or purchased by them which could explain this tremendous surge. Neither had they recruited a bunch of whiz kids who could have been responsible for the same. The analysts were baffled beyond belief. What was this secret weapon that Talati Industries had acquired?

Both the competitors and the analysts doubled their spies and quadrupled their efforts, hoping to break the jigsaw of the enigma of Talati Industries. In their desperation, the analysts went beyond boardroom strategy and met employees at the grass-root level, hoping to find some clue there. They asked the employees what had changed so drastically at Talati Industries, recently. All the answers were the same, "There is a passbook which we have all been given. We can accumulate points if we do **GOOD DEEDS** of our choice, in our free time."

"Could there really be any substance to this nonsense?" the analysts asked themselves and one another, "Is it really possible that these phenomenal rises in profit can be attributed to some new-fangled, goody-goody, touchy-feely Human Resource initiative? Can there be any amount of truth in this fairy-tale we keep hearing, churned out by all the employees of Talati Industries we speak to?"

These analysts being used to deal with hard figures and cold cash, were extremely difficult nuts to crack. All the more when it came to understand the softer side of management. These people's jobs and lives revolved around numbers. If the share price of a firm consistently went up or down, it was their job to nail it and tie up this movement with something tangible - something from their world that they could only comprehend and explain in the terms they were used to dealing with.

With no other answer forthcoming, and the profit graph of Talati Industries showing no sign of relaxing, the analysts and competitors were forced to take these stories seriously. They had to find the connection between the social work and commercial success at Talati Industries. Everyone was sure that there was something that was being done differently in a positive way, which accounted for the consistent rise in share prices.

> "A man's true wealth is
> the good he does in this world."
> – Prophet Muhammad

The analysts knew very well that the stock market would not lie for such an extended period. The figures were definitely a projection of reality, no matter how hypothetical they looked. On further investigation, the analysts found out that it wasn't only the stock prices that had soared at Talati Industries. Their productivity had increased, conflicts between workers and management had become non-existent, and their customers seemed more than satisfied, thereby reducing complaints.

The analysts and competitors now had no option but to put intense efforts to identify what the **GOOD DEED PASSBOOK** was all about and how it worked. Of course, Talati Industries had made no secret of the initiative - indeed, with hundreds of thousands of their employees involved, it could hardly be kept a secret. Also, neither did Rohinton Talati, nor the management feel the need to keep these measures a secret.

Despite the openness about the scheme and the passbook, the analysts and competitors took really long to find out exactly what was happening. This proved an often forgotten truth - *the answers which are obvious are often ignored.*

Also, people who had grown studying and putting their faith primarily in figures and balance sheets, would surely find it difficult to shift gaze and focus on the softer aspects that impact businesses. After all, in the modern management context - soft is the new hard.

> "Management is nothing more than motivating other people."
> – Lee Iacocca

Normally, when a new employee joins an organisation, for a few days or weeks he views the organisation and it's functioning from the eyes and perspective of an outsider. Once that initial period is over, the employee becomes immersed in the culture and adopts the mindset prevalent in the organisation. The same happens when analysts and competitors who are stuck in a certain mindset, which is the default standard of the industry, view events through their microscopic lens. But, when evidence piles up to the contrary, they have no option but to shift gears and view things through new lenses.

This is exactly when these experts in the field of finance, business and analytics realized; that maybe, just maybe, there was an element of substance in the apparently unrelated things that people were talking about at Talati Industries. These people were novices in the field of human behavior, motivation and psychology.

The growth and success of Talati Industries due to the implementation of the **GOOD DEED PASSBOOK,** was becoming more and more difficult to ignore. They had also overshot the expectations of the market by miles, and ended their quarter with unbelievable numbers. The stocks of Talati Industries had a rise of over two hundred percent, which also made them one of the top hundred companies in the world.

Happÿness
bank

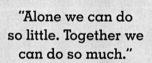

"Alone we can do
so little. Together we
can do so much."

- Hellen Keller

The
Happyness
Bank

It was that time of the year when business awards were being finalised, and the jury was on the lookout for offering awards to innovative organisations. Notably, Talati Industries was given the best coverage in every source of media possible, highlighting the company's new way of working and the benefits received from it. It wasn't a surprise when the most prestigious award of them all - *The Modern Times Award for Best Innovative Business Practice*, was proudly received by Rohinton Talati, at the hands of none other than The Honorable Prime Minister of India.

India had a dynamic new Prime Minister in the Chair, who was determined to take India to her rightful place - right at the top of the table of nations, in the parameters which mattered the most. This new Prime Minister, Honorable Mr. Narottam Mehta, had a vision in which he saw India emerging as:

- A developed and economically powerful country that had charted its own destiny.
- A country where illiteracy and poverty were a thing of the past.
- A clean country where disease was under control.
- A country where people were skilled and empowered.
- A country where the people were united with a common purpose.
- A country whose products were acceptable as quality offerings throughout the world.

As Mr. Narottam Mehta handed over the prestigious award to Rohinton Talati, he praised the brilliant initiative that Talati Industries had undertaken. Being a highly intuitive man, he recognized the tremendous potential that Rohinton's idea had, as soon as he heard about it. Hence, Mr. Mehta immediately requested Rohinton and his core team to guide him and the Government, to initiate the **GOOD DEED** project on a national level.

Rohinton's happiness knew no bounds. This opportunity was beyond his wildest dreams. When he had first visited Gauraj Nagar, little had he anticipated the great heights to which this simple idea with its humongous potential to unleash the latent power of goodness in people, could reach. Rohinton thanked the Prime Minister profusely, as he graciously accepted the offer and the honour.

Great things were expected from the action-oriented Prime Minister. The people of India not only wanted change, but they longed for consistent **POSITIVE PROGRESS.** Narottam Mehta was a visionary who walked his strong talk. A man grown up from living at the bottom, he had proved himself to be a sterling success as far as economic progress and upliftment of the masses was concerned, in his home state. The people of India had now allowed him to govern them at a national level, and they expected him to deliver.

Narottam Mehta believed in concrete action and not just lip - service. He had recently won the elections with a thumping victory, and the whole nation was looking up to him to guide them to heights previously unattained. India, with its billion-plus population had been plagued ever since Independence, from all the possible problems a developing nation could possibly suffer from. **These problems being multiple and humongous, included:**

- Low literacy levels including the lack of basic, quality primary education.
- Skewed development and growth pattern where only a few cities were developed, and hence over-crowded.
- Insufficient employment as most people lacked practical, employable job-related skills.
- Extreme poverty in large sections of the society.

The Happyness Bank

- Lower quantity and quality of industrial output than it deserved to have as per its size, resources and population.
- Rampant corruption at all levels; leaving the common man exhausted just getting even simple paper-work done.
- Lack of quality health care.
- High crime rates.
- Communal hatred and the existence of vote-bank politics.
- Inter-state conflicts over even sharing basic resources such as water.
- Linguistic divide.

> "Nearly all men can stand adversity, but,
> if you want to test a man's character, give him power."
> –Abraham Lincoln

For the past sixty-eight odd years post-Independence, various governments had come and gone. Each had rolled out several policies to apparently assist and uplift the masses. These policies ranged from providing free food to the poor to the waiver of loans. The intentions of the policy-framers may have been good, but most of the policies had failed miserably. It was also a well-known fact that most of these policies of mass appeal were formulated more with the idea of garnering votes, and therefore clinging to power. They had less to do with really helping to uplift the poor.

The nation thus, also suffered from the ugly reality of vote-bank politics. It had so far proved to be almost impossible for a single government to effectively reach out to the poor and uneducated people in a meaningful way. In fact, most of the schemes which had been launched with the expressed aim of helping the poor, had badly backfired. Providing free food to the needy and poor seemed a noble objective, but doing so repeatedly actually created more poverty, dependency and excess population. Now, that this section of society was assured of getting free food for nothing, they happily produced even more children that naturally added to the population which had to be provided with free food.

These schemes also made many of the poor recipients lazy. Due to the provision of free food, they eventually became comfortable with not working. This dole prevented them from being motivated to develop essential skills to support themselves and their families, and contribute to the growth of the Indian economy. Also, due to the fact that corruption was rampant, not even fifteen percent of the funds allotted for these schemes reached the intended beneficiaries. The bulk was neatly siphoned off by middle-men and people-in-charge. It was, therefore, impossible for the government to effectively help the poor and guide them on a path which would make them self-sufficient rather than becoming a liability to the nation. Considering all these short-comings in the policies and schemes, India needed a radical new idea to convert the country's greatest current liability into its most valuable long-term asset - the poor and illiterate.

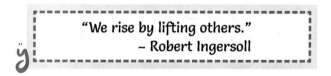

> "We rise by lifting others."
> – Robert Ingersoll

Once the award ceremony was over, the Prime Minister began to think intensively. He had always been on the lookout for that one idea that could help the country move forward, from the sluggish pace at which it had inched ahead since independence. As he dwelled deeper and studied Talati Industries' new scheme and its concept in detail, he spent a couple of sleepless nights mulling over how he could possibly implement this idea on a nation-wide scale.

The Prime Minister, only having the best interests of the nation at heart, didn't waste much time in formulating and elaborating the **BANK of GOOD KARMA** on a nation-wide level. He decided to give the chiseled new idea a new name - THE Happyness Bank, dedicating it to the people of India. He eventually formed a committee that would look into the creation and implementation of THE Happyness Bank. Narottam Mehta invited the

CEOs of all nationalized and large private banks alike to be a part of the initial committee. Rohinton Talati was also on this committee, as it was the implementation in his organization that had sparked it to reach a larger level.

The committee members met with the head honchos and captains of industry across the nation, who would eventually become important movers for fine-tuning and implementing this concept. These individuals were requested to get involved along with their organisations, and participate in the implementation of the Happyness Bank at the scale that the Prime Minister had in mind.

The Prime Minister based the scheme on the foundation that every bank and large corporate house would allocate a certain amount of money for Corporate Social Responsibility, under the new CSR Act. Also, put together, these banks and corporate houses covered more than ninety-five percent of the country, in terms of geographical reach. Hence, these entities were requested to support this idea all the more, by diverting some of the already allocated resources that they had set aside for CSR activities, towards the Happyness Bank. Because of this, the banks and corporate houses did not have to allocate any additional resources to participate in this scheme.

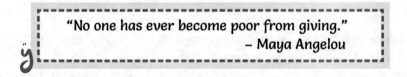

> *"No one has ever become poor from giving."*
> *– Maya Angelou*

The idea that the Prime Minister had conceptualised and formulated through his fertile mind was brilliant, since it would create a **WIN-WIN** situation for all stake-holders, and solve all the prevailing problems of the nation. This would give India a new trajectory of development, growth and prosperity.

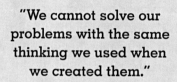

"We cannot solve our
problems with the same
thinking we used when
we created them."

- Albert Einstein

Action
and
Implementation

The first *avatar* of the **GOOD DEED PASSBOOK** had been triggered off at Gauraj Nagar by Atul Upadhay, changing the face of a grief stricken village. In the second *avatar*, Rohinton Talati polished it further and metamorphosed the workings of his multiple organisations. In the third *avatar* of the **GOOD DEED PASSBOOK,** the idea was further refurbished by India's new Prime Minister.

In a simple yet effective manner, the Prime Minister asked each bank to allocate a small ten by ten feet space, at each of their branches. A desk would be manned by one or two people, who would give the **HAPPYNESS PASSBOOK** to citizens that applied to be a part of the Happyness Bank scheme. A set of two lists would also be provided as attachments along with this passbook.

LIST ONE would contain a summation of all the GOOD DEEDS that a person could perform. This list would initially be decided and formulated by the committee, and then updated on a quarterly basis, based on the evidence offered by the **HAPPYNESS PASSBOOK** holders. To begin with, sixteen vital categories of **GOOD DEEDS** were made, keeping a national perspective in mind. Each of these sixteen categories had one or more activities listed under it. For example, volunteering to teach in schools and colleges, blood and organ donation, etc. Participating in each of these categories could win a person a certain number of points, which would then be recorded in his or her **HAPPYNESS PASSBOOK**.

LIST TWO would contain tie-ups the committee would establish with organisations such as NGOs, hospitals, schools, colleges, etc. These organisations would cater to the categories of good deeds listed out in **LIST ONE.** For example, if one of the **GOOD DEEDS** listed under a particular category was to donate blood, then **LIST TWO** would have names and contact details of hospitals or blood banks across the country, listed state-wise. The person who wished to donate blood could then go to that place and complete his or her deed. In short, **LIST ONE** would contain a list of **GOOD DEEDS** that could be done, and **LIST TWO** would contain the contact details of where these **GOOD DEEDS** could be performed.

> "Anything that is of value
> in life only multiplies when it is given."
> – Deepak Chopra

The procedure for opening an account at the Happyness Bank was kept as simple as possible. Any Indian citizen above the age of five could open an account with this bank. All they would have to do is, visit any bank branch that had a Happyness Bank counter, and enroll themselves by filling up a simple form with basic details. Furthermore, if someone relocated within India, they could continue to use their existing account, as all accounts and branches would be linked nationwide. The Prime Minster also decided that the **HAPPYNESS PASSBOOK** would become one of the primary documents for identification purposes.

The passbook would be sponsored by the bank that issued it, and given to the account holder at absolutely no cost. The bank would have to bear the cost of printing the passbook, and its corresponding two lists. Additionally, the issuing bank could use the **HAPPYNESS PASSBOOK** as a marketing tool for its own service offerings. For example, if someone opened a **HAPPYNESS ACCOUNT** from the State Bank of India, this bank would have the prerogative to advertise on it.

The issuing bank would have to update the passbook when the account holders came to get their **GOOD DEEDS** registered and recorded. Initially, one or two of the bank employees would be trained to handle the Happyness Bank counter. However, the managing of these counters would later be done by appointed Happyness Bank volunteers, who would do it as part of their own **GOOD DEEDS**, and earn points for the same.

> "Christmas is forever, and not for just one day.
> Loving, sharing and giving are not to put away like bells,
> lights and tinsel, in some box upon a shelf. The good you
> do for others is the good you do for yourself."
> – Norman Wesley Brooks

Happÿness
bank

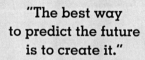

"The best way
to predict the future
is to create it."

- Abraham Lincoln

The
Good Deed
Lists

The Prime Minister's committee spent several weeks on designing and formulating the initial **GOOD DEED** list to be used nation-wide. The committee divided the list of activities they had finalised into various categories. Each category encompassed the **GOOD DEEDS** and activities that would fall under that category. Also, depending upon the nature of **GOOD DEEDS**, each deed would be given points ranging from a minimum of 1 to a maximum of 5, per year.

The first list which was called **LIST ONE,** was divided into sixteen categories for convenience and segregating similar kinds of activities together, in order to award points specifically to that activity. This eliminated the duplication of points too. For example, all activities related to **Monetary Donation** to various causes would be segregated under one category, and this category could win a person a maximum of 5 points.

Therefore, a rich person could not garner more points by subscribing to various monetary donation activities. He would get a maximum of 5 points a year for any money donating-related activity, irrespective of how much he donated. This scheme would thus, take care of the fact that people with varying incomes would be at par, and no one could secure more points for themselves merely by donating more money.

The number of points secured by an individual would depend on the nature of the activity, the benefits accruing from this activity, and the efforts required by the individual to perform that activity. Even though, this was an area of subjectivity, a common-sense and practical approach was adopted, based on the common experience of a reasonable man who would have to perform that activity. For example, naturally though blood donation was an important and vital activity, more points would be given for a person donating bone-marrow than a person donating blood, as donating bone-marrow was a far more difficult, time and energy consuming activity.

Some activities were one-time activities - points could be earned for these only once in a lifetime. For example, if a person signed up to donate his eyes post his demise, he would be rewarded with 5 points. That would be the end of earning points with regard to the activity of that particular organ donation. Some activities would be considered as on-going activities in which a person could earn 5 points from them every year.

For example, activities related to areas such as volunteering time to teach, voluntary work with an orphanage or an old-age home, donating money to worthy causes, etc. This could secure a person 5 points every year, whenever such activities would be carried out.

The idea of keeping an upper-limit of 5 points per category each year was to ensure that people were encouraged to try their hand at performing new types of good deeds, where they could further secure more points. People would hence, not restrict themselves to doing only one type of good deed which would otherwise happen, if they could secure unlimited points for the same.

The list also tried to maintain religious equality. Under the category of **RELIGIOUS GOOD-DEEDS**, activities relating to Hindus, Muslims, Christians and people from other religions were considered, so as to give people from all religions, an opportunity to earn points under this activity. The good-deeds under this category could involve activities such as volunteering for *langar* at Gurudwaras, Christians attending Church services, and so on. The idea of offering points under this category was to motivate people to stay connected to a Divine Source. This would hopefully make a person more spiritual and more considerate to others.

> "The willingness to share does not make one charitable; it makes one free."
> – Robert Brault

Today a lot of people want to do good work but they don't know what to do, how to go about it and where to go and do it. This is often where people get stuck as they don't know who to approach, nor do they know if the assistance they give will be of any genuine benefit to its recipients. This is where **LIST TWO** would come in use. It would complement **LIST ONE** by providing a comprehensive nation-wide list of names and contact details of organisations that had tie-ups with the Happyness Bank.

The Good Deed Lists

Some kind of authentic evidence was also requested to avail the points for performing the **GOOD DEEDS**. This, from an individual's perspective was important, in order to make sure that his good efforts would not be wasted by donating money, or volunteering his time and effort to organisations that were not genuine.

Thus, the government created a nation-wide database of authenticated organisations, NGOs, hospitals and the like, where activities mentioned in **LIST ONE** could be performed and then recorded at the Happyness Banks' counters.

All the organisations mentioned in this list would be credible ones, thus, the person performing a **GOOD DEED** would be assured that whatever he was doing, whether donating money or giving free skill-training; his time, effort and money was being put to good and genuine use. This was essential since, for decades together, many so-called charitable organisations had been prosecuted for unfair and illegal practices. Due to this, there was a lot of mistrust amongst the general public with regards to credibility of such organisations. This was one of the major reasons why many people, who would otherwise have liked to volunteer their time, or donate their money to good causes, hesitated from doing so. **LIST TWO** being formulated and audited first hand by the Indian Government, would therefore build trust amongst the people subscribing to the Happyness Bank.

The organisations mentioned in **LIST TWO** would maintain records of the activities done by account-holders of the Happyness Bank, hence, a double-entry type of system of recording would be achieved. This would ensure a real activity being completed by an individual, together with earning suitable points. Chances of manipulation by any individual to record more points than they deserved would thus, be minimised.

LIST TWO would give a person opportunities to undertake voluntary activities which they always wanted to do, but did not have any source of genuine information in order to carry them out. For example, if a person always wanted to teach his skill of computers free of cost, he now had a list of genuine organisations where he could teach this skill to truly deserving people, and also avail of points for his efforts.

Happyness Bank

If a person wanted to donate blood, now he had a list of genuine blood banks where he could donate it and he would be assured that his activity was really helping someone and that he was not a part of some scam. If someone wanted to donate money for a particular cause, let's say a girl child. The person now, had contact details of many organisations with a credible background, where he was ensured that his money would be used for the cause he supported, and where he did not have to worry about misuse of his donation as all these organisations would be authenticated by the government and subjected to strict audit.

With these lists, one could be introduced to new areas of **GOODNESS** which they had never thought of personally participating in before. For example, carpenters, plumbers, truck-drivers, electricians, air-condition repair and maintenance persons, etc., could teach and pass on their skill to the newcomers of the trade, and thus, earn points for the same. Therefore, these two lists put together opened new possibilities and areas of good work which people were unaware about or had not considered earlier. Categories of assistance that were not thought of before, now became new windows of opportunity

Once enrolled as a member of the Happyness Bank and receiving the **HAPPYNESS PASSBOOK**, that person could immediately begin with doing his share of **GOOD DEEDS,** and earn points for the same. The points earned would keep adding up throughout one's lifetime. At every slab of additional 50 points earned, that person would be eligible for a reward, from any organisation that wished to reward the person for his achievement. The milestone slabs were therefore 50, 100, 150, 200, and so on.

All kinds of business organisations and corporate entities, large or small, were excited with the announcement of the **HAPPYNESS PASSBOOK**. They were more than willing to offer discounts and other goodies to people who were performing **GOOD DEEDS** as a goodwill gesture, which also brought them much needed positive publicity. Also, this created new business opportunities for them by attracting new customers, to try out the products and services offered by their organization.

Corporate houses also started announcing schemes where people who had accumulated a certain number points could avail of certain discounts, privileges, products, services and facilities. These schemes would be totally up to the corporates to formulate. The facilities, benefits and discounts provided by the corporate entities to the **HAPPYNESS PASSBOOK** holders, would also be acceptable as deductions for corporates under the new Corporate Social Responsibility Act.

The Government also in its own right, decided to provide benefits and facilities as points and **REWARDS**. These would be in the form of an additional half percent in the individual's Public Provident Fund or a Public Bank Fixed Deposit. Railway reservations and other such government services would also be escalated faster for the point holders.

This was the first time ever, in the history of the world, that a government on a national level was **RECOGNIZING, RECORDING and REWARDING GOOD DEEDS** in a structured manner. Unfortunately, by default, the job of governments is restricted to only recording and punishing the bad, rather than recognizing and rewarding the good. This shift in mindset from the negative to the **POSITIVE** itself made the concept of the Happyness Bank, a **REVOLUTIONARY GAME-CHANGER** in the way that the government was perceived by the citizens.

(An elaborate list of suggested categories and the corresponding points has been tabulated at the end of the book in Appendix 2)

Happÿness Bank

Passbook

The bank that changed the world

NAME. **Rahul Singh**	ADDRESS. **Mumbai**
ACCOUNT NO. **HB-369**	
GENDER. **Male**	EMAIL. rahulsingh@ky2.com
DATE of BIRTH. **28/02/1972**	CONTACT NO.
PLACE of ISSUE. **Mumbai**	
DATE of ISSUE. **01/12/2016**	

Date	Activity	Category No.	Points	Stamp
30/6/2017	Filed income tax on time.	14	05	
15/8/2017	Free teaching in government college.	01	03	
20/9/2017	Participated in cleaning Versova beach.	05	02	
12/12/2017	Voted for State Legislature.	13	05	
20/8/2018	Volunteered for Kerela Relief Work.	06	05	

The Good Deed Lists

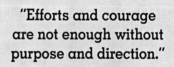

"Efforts and courage
are not enough without
purpose and direction."

- John F Kennedy

Freedom, Growth & Prosperity

Prime Minister Narottam Mehta selected the auspicious Indian Independence Day, 15th August, to announce and officially inaugurate the commencement of THE Happyness Bank. He assured the nation that this scheme would bring about independence from poverty, illiteracy, ill-health, and unemployment. This scheme would truly fulfill the dreams of our valiant freedom-fighters who had envisioned a free and prosperous India, for which they had willingly laid down their own lives. The Prime Minister mentioned amid loud cheers of gathered multitudes, that the ultimate goal of the Happyness Bank, as

its name suggested, was to make India a happy, healthy and prosperous nation.

As soon as the announcement was made and the scheme was rolled out, the business community almost instantly went into a frenzy, as they grasped and understood the grandeur of this scheme. They knew this scheme would help them grow to previously unattainable heights. Restaurants, airlines, retails outlets, hotels, etc., all started to formulate different kinds of schemes to offer people. Slabs of rewards with various discount-offers, combination-offers, and choice of goodies were also chalked out. All this attracted people to work harder, earn more points and avail the facilities and discounts offered.

A leading airline immediately announced that they would offer a 10% discount to all those who had earned 50 points, and a 25% discount for those who had earned over a 100 points, on certain routes and in certain seasons. Some airlines even announced a 50% discount to upgrade to business class, for people with 50 points and more, and 100% free upgrade to business class, for people who had earned over a 100 points, on certain flights and on certain sectors. Free food with an economy class fare for persons who had earned 50 points and above, was also offered by some airlines.

As per **LIST ONE**, people would get points for visiting their renowned religious places. Hence, the railways started offering special discounts to people wanting to visit these places, as per the list. They also offered priority in reservation for travel to those who had earned above 50 and 100 points.

A leading bank, on hearing about the scheme, immediately announced a 0.25% discount on home and car loans, to people who had earned over 50 points. A 0.40% discount for people who had earned over a 100 points was also offered. Some banks also increased the interest rate offered on fixed deposits by 0.25%, for people who had earned over 50 points, and by 0.35% for people with a 100 points and above.

Restaurants started offering attractive discounts and combination meal offers for people having a certain number of points in their **HAPPYNESS PASSBOOK**. Similarly, millions of retail outlets and e-commerce websites also began offering various discounts and schemes, for all those people who had earned a certain number of points.

Automobile manufacturers also offered discounts on sale and services on various models for people with a certain number of points. Similarly, organisations across the spectrum of goods and services, also rushed to participate in this scheme and take advantage of it. After all, there was a great amount of goodwill they could earn by being part of one of the largest schemes the world had ever seen.

Even the Indian Government wasn't left behind. They announced an increase of 0.25% on the Public Provident Fund scheme for a period of three years, for people who had earned over 50 points. Also, the government was able to rope in leading Bollywood film-stars and popular celebrities, who agreed to meet and give photo opportunities to people reaching the initial milestones of 50 points.

The Indian Government further announced that people convicted of offenses, would now get an opportunity to reduce their terms of punishment by earning a sufficient number of points through their **GOOD DEEDS.** Thus, this scheme ushered a new era of thinking within the system, where a person convicted would be motivated to do **GOOD WORK,** and in exchange would be rewarded by reduction of his term, depending on the points garnered. It had long been the argument of many, that human beings are victims of **circumstances**, and however, grievous the crime committed, there must be methods designed for people to get an opportunity to redeem themselves.

The Prime Minister involved himself in the Happyness Bank scheme too. To kick-start this on the right footing, generate maximum enthusiasm and enrollment, he announced that the first thousand individuals that enrolled with the Happyness Bank, and achieved 50 points in a certain number of days, would be invited for tea with him, at his official residence.

> "With every deed you are sowing a seed,
> though the harvest you may not see."
> – Ella Wheeler Wilcox

The beauty of this scheme was that rewards were being offered to people not because they were born in a particular family, owned a particular credit card, or that they traveled frequently. They were being rewarded only for being good human beings and doing good work.

A healthy competition between people emerged, to see who could get more points, motivating themselves to do even better. The public-spirited competition inspired people to nurture their good side, and once they did this often enough, being and doing good became a habit. This habit would then spread to others, eventually leading to a virtuous, happy and evolved society.

Freedom, Growth Prosperity

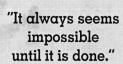

"It always seems
impossible
until it is done."

- Nelson Mandela

The Chain
Reaction of
Goodness

The implementation of the Happyness Bank and the **HAPPYNESS PASSBOOK** had a miraculous effect on the entire country. The positive results went even beyond the wildest dreams of the Prime Minister, who himself was a very positive-minded person. The Prime Minister's philosophy of, *"Every human being has a lot of goodness inside him. We must do something so as to motivate him to act on that goodness,"* had succeeded stupendously.

A chain-reaction of goodness had begun which had enveloped the whole country like the bright sunshine on a lovely summer morning. Within a span of two short years, India leapt forward more than it had in the past six decades post-Independence. The results were unbelievable. Over two hundred million people had opened an account with the Happyness Bank, just within the first two years of its commencement.

Benefits due to **CATEGORY I** of activities related to teaching, were at the level of school education, millions of school-children from low-income backgrounds received free and better quality education from volunteers. In the Indian culture, a woman going out to work and earning money was still not looked upon as a good thing. If a woman decided to teach for free at a nearby school or college, it was acceptable by her family and in-laws. Therefore, this scheme unleashed a power more potent than all the gold owned by the Reserve Bank of India - the power of millions of educated but non-working women.

Millions of educated women who were just spending their time at home and not contributing to the work-force or the national economy in any meaningful manner, now joined the work force, and that too without accepting any payment in return. At the same time, they garnered valuable points which ultimately helped them get various rewards, thereby indirectly helping them get many benefits. They were also not hurting any cultural sentiments.

At the college level, millions of students got the benefit of attending free seminars and getting valuable tips from successful business leaders. Normally, it would take a great deal of effort to get these business tycoons to take out time and teach college students and share their experiences.

But, under the Happyness Bank concept, business leaders were motivated to garner as many points as possible. Therefore, in a reversal of roles, the business leaders were now interested in doing their **GOOD DEEDS,** and getting them entered in the **HAPPYNESS PASSBOOK.**

As a result of this massive entry into the supply-side of education, the illiteracy rate in the nation dropped drastically, raising the mean education-level of an Indian citizen, significantly. Education is the cornerstone of any developed society. India is also known as the birthplace of the first universities in the world - Nalanda and Taxila. Now, India was speeding back to meet its appointment with its past glory; of once again becoming a highly educated and intelligent society.

Due to participation in **CATEGORY 15**, i.e. vocational training, millions of fully-abled men and women, who previously did not have the finances or an opportunity to learn any vocational and job-oriented skill, now became semi-skilled or fully-skilled by availing on-the-job-training. Existing plumbers, carpenters, cooks, truck-drivers, nurses, electricians, house-hold helps, all enrolled themselves to impart on-the-job training to people from other cities and states. The other city or state clause was inserted to prevent the Happyness Bank account holders or the volunteers, from feeling insecure about their own jobs, and also prevent them from creating their own competition in their own geographical area of work. This was a psychological factor which had to be considered.

> "Only a life lived in the
> service to others is worth living."
> – Albert Einstein

Earning more points also became prestigious for the rich and powerful. Well, as long as it benefited all the stakeholders involved, there was nothing wrong in motivating these successful people by offering points, even if it was through the channel of ego and prestige. At the level of middle and senior management, thousands of Indians got training on leadership concepts and the successful running of companies, by leading experts.

The Chain Reaction of Goodness

India having a vast population and a huge requirement for people for doing labour-intensive jobs, had very few people joining the work force in a productive manner, since they had no opportunity and money to acquire those particular skill-sets. As a harsh example, thousands of young girls in poor regions of the country would be forced into prostitution as they had no job-oriented skills, while at the same time thousands of house helps, adult caretakers and nurses were required in the metropolitan cities of New Delhi, Mumbai, Chennai, Bengaluru and Kolkata.

There was a complete mismatch between the demand and supply of skilled labour, in many parts of India. Category 15 related to of skill development helped young girls with no formal education, master important skills such as cooking, cleaning, child-care, adult-care, and household chores. In this manner, these young girls became eligible for placement as house helps in metropolitan cities, for handsome salaries, and also attained a roof over their heads. Thus, this category converted thousands of unemployed and illiterate young girls and boys, from being labeled as a liability and worthless, to skilled and useful human assets. This category embodied the Chinese philosophy of - *Give a man a fish and you feed him for a day; teach him how to fish and you feed him for a lifetime.*" From being victims of circumstances, the youth became masters of their destiny.

> "You must not lose faith in humanity.
> Humanity is an ocean; if a few drops of the ocean
> are dirty, the entire ocean does not become dirty."
> – Mahatma Gandhi

Money coming in from donations in **CATEGORY 2,** was channelized into the skill factories that became self-sufficient over a period of time. Every year, the target was a million skilled people passing through the doors of these skill factories. Someone having one skill could also enrol for learning another.

Due to **CATEGORY 3**, the blood banks were fully stocked with blood of all blood groups. The shortage of blood supply which was common at one point of time, completely disappeared. In fact, a list of people having rare blood groups were archived, and at a moment's notice, they could be summoned for donating blood. The blood donors now willingly and helped by donating blood, as their good action was being **RECORDED**, **RECOGNISED** and **REWARDED**. Thousands also signed up to donate kidneys, heart and liver and eyes, as and when they would pass away. This unprecedented sign up assured that in a few years, thousands of Indians would practically get a new life.

Crores of rupees were collected, which under government supervision and audit, were spent in the areas of health, skill, education, and infrastructural development. These funds gave further impetus to the Happyness Bank scheme. Thousands of doctors, lawyers and chartered accountants signed up to provide free services to candidates who had enrolled themselves with the Happyness Bank. For example, heart surgeons, who were not accessible to the poor for surgeries like bypass and angioplasty, now performed at least ten surgeries free of cost on the enrolled candidates. Lawyers fought a free fixed number of cases and chartered accountants offered their knowledge of accounts and tax planning at no cost to the Happyness Bank account holders.

Being a democracy, using the power of votes was seen as one of the most important aspects of a constantly developing India. However, many people did not give due importance to elections and voting. The government had tried to motivate people to vote through various advertising campaigns, but although it built awareness, there was hardly any increase in the number of voters. Due to category no 13, people were highly motivated, and an unbelievable 90% voters turn out resulted in many parts of the country.

Thousands of unemployed youth got on-the-job training in labor-intensive professions, and were able to start earning their livelihoods in a respectable and decent manner. From being labeled as poor, worthless and incapable of ever rising beyond a certain point in society, through this training, many of the youth now dreamt of travelling to foreign lands like Dubai, Abu Dhabi, Muscat, Singapore, etc., where there was a huge demand for such skilled labor. This in turn also brought back precious foreign exchange for the nation.

The Chain Reaction of Goodness

"A tree is known by its fruit;
a man by his deeds. A good deed is never lost;
he who sows courtesy reaps friendship,
and he who plants kindness gathers love."
– Saint Basil

Happÿness
bank

"Every time
you do a good deed,
you shine the light a little
farther into the dark.
And the thing is, when you're
gone that light is going to
keep shining on,
pushing the back."

- Charles de Lint

The World
Takes Notice

For well over half a century, India has been looked down upon like a step-child. One of the reasons for this was, the elite countries of the world had their own set of parameters, indices and metrics to evaluate and ascertain which countries should be admitted into the 'who's who' club, of the top-most nations of the world. The parameters always boil down to money in some form or the other.

The United Nations also had its own parameters to evaluate what it terms as sustainable development. They rightly focus on areas such as eradication of poverty, reduction of pollution, strengthening health systems, education, good governance, economic development and the like. Under these broad headers lie specific indicators and metrics such as, households with access to electricity or sources of fuel, access to hygienic sanitation facilities, crime rate, mortality rate, life expectancy at birth, immunisation of children, nutritional status, vulnerability to contagious diseases, enrolment in primary and secondary education, adult literacy rate, employable skills, air quality, area covered by forestation, water quantity and quality; economic factors such as GDP, savings rate, employment rate, share of women in non-agricultural employment; internet usage, waste management, access to transportation, and the like. Quite a comprehensive and exhaustive and a well thought out list to measure the living standards of the population of a nation.

Just before the Happyness Bank concept and passbook were initiated by the Prime Minister, India despite its best efforts over the years, had remained sluggish on most of these parameters and metrics. One of the major reasons for this was, India, with its vast population did not stand united. The people divided themselves on the basis of caste, religion, language and even ideologies. Therefore, the power of unity which should have come from a billion-plus people standing together, never materialized.

> "Great nations write their autobiographies in three manuscripts – the book of their deeds, the book of their words and the book of their art."
> – John Ruskin

The winds of change were shifting the tide nevertheless. Within a span of two short years of the Happyness Bank being implemented, the metrics on which India's performance had been dismal, demonstrated a marked upswing -

- Contagious diseases were down manifold
- Crime rates and incidents of terrorism were lowered
- There were more girls in school than ever before
- Vastly increased percentage of households had secured access to hygienic sanitation, potable drinking water, and cooking fuel
- Unemployment rate was lowered. New small-scale businesses were being launched and successfully run
- Industrial production was up. Industrial conflicts and disputes were almost non-existent
- Tax collection had increased
- The GDP of the nation had increased quarter-upon-quarter in those two years
- People were pledging to donate their organs and lining up for blood donation in large numbers

The leading developed nations of the world eventually started noticing the drastic sea of positive change that India was going through. It almost seemed magical and beyond logic to most of them. They also knew that there had been no major financial or economic policy changes announced by the Reserve Bank of India, which could have resulted in this magnanimous change in the country and its people. Economists were left scratching their heads too as they tried all they could, to understand the cause of the surge in positive growth, on almost every parameter that mattered.

Behavioral experts and psychologists were asked to help, and identify the link between what India had been just over two years ago, and what it was currently. Some of these experts suggested that Indians had started becoming more of their true selves - co-operative beings, as opposed to competitive beings. From using closed fists to push others down, they had started lending hands to pull people up.

The World Takes Notice

On further research, it was found that the same motivation that the recording of GOOD DEEDS in an earthquake stricken small town of Gauraj Nagar had driven people out of depression, soaring them to greater heights, was the same motivation that pushed a large group of companies - The Talati Industries, to become one of the world's best companies. This idea had greatly inspired the Prime Minister of India, Mr. Narottam Mehta, who refurbished it in an even bigger way to implement it across the country, which eventually changed the entire face of the nation.

India was well and truly on the move, rapidly surging ahead. This time it was not just a feel-good factor which made people say it, but the facts and figures which did. When facts and figures speak, the world takes notice.

"Most people
don't believe something
can happen until it
already has. That's
not stupidity or weakness,
that's just human nature"

- Max Brooks

The Sceptics have their Say

"If it were so easy to bring about positive change, someone would have done it long ago.

"People will join the scheme just to take advantage."

"People are selfish. They will only give something if they're getting something more in return.

"It will never last. It's just the novelty of the scheme that's making it work."

"The government is focusing on this scheme to get people's mind off the real issues."

"This is interfering with the Law of Karma. Only The Law of Karma has the right to reward for good deeds done."

These were some of the comments which emanated from the mouths of the sceptics, the nay-sayers, the armchair critics, the pessimists and the ones who always saw the small black dot on the white sheet of paper. These were the ones who would expertly find flaws even in the Creation of the Universe itself.

Yet, it takes all kinds of people to make a world. Edward De Bono, the master thinker, calls such people as the ones wearing the 'black hat.' They always see the worst in everything, and their stance too serves a purpose. If such people did not exist, then we probably wouldn't have brakes on our cars, no early warning systems for earthquakes and tsunamis, or maybe even no locks on our doors. These are the set of people who ensure that an idea has all its weak points, and is thrashed out before it becomes generally acceptable.

> **"Skepticism is the first step towards truth."**
> – Denis Diderot

The government naturally wanted the Happyness Bank scheme to succeed, because the Prime Minister, and almost the entire Cabinet felt that this was the solution they had been looking for, to rid India of all her ills and put her on the rightful path to glory.

Therefore, the Prime Minister called on a press conference where he personally addressed a large crowd giving Atul due credit for the seed of the idea, and Rohinton Talati the credit for carrying the idea forward at a corporate level.

Prime Minister Narottam Mehta requested all present to voice their doubts. The clarity would help people implement the idea in a much better way, and also help the country to keep improving itself. "Brothers and sisters," began the Prime Minister, "You rightly ask. If it were so simple to solve all our problems, someone would have done this a long time ago. Your question is valid. To this query of yours, I humble quote our sacred scripture, wherein it is said - *Samay se pehle aur bhagya se adhik kissi ko kuch nahi milta. (Before time and more than one is destined, no-one gets anything.)*

"Everything, my dear brothers and sisters, unfolds at its own divine time. The time was probably ripe right now, for the Happyness Bank to come into all lives. Maybe, all the pain and struggle that we have been put through, was to prepare us for the wonderful gift God was going to give us in the form of this wonderful idea. Some of you may also feel that not everyone will join the scheme with a genuine intention of doing good from their hearts. They may do it just to gain points and rewards. If so, then I say let them do so by all means. As long as they are doing good and helping those in need, the purpose is served."

"When we go on our pilgrimages to pray, don't most of us ask for some type of reward? Don't people take all kinds of *mannats (prayer requests)*, keep fasts or even vow to sacrifice something so they receive something they truly desire? Most of us are well aware of the psychological fact - do any activity for twenty-one consecutive days, and that activity becomes a habit. This is true not only for actions but also in terms of thought. So initially though an individual may commence doing good deeds to secure points and rewards, when he continues doing good, it will eventually become a habit. This will entrench itself into the very core of his inner-self.

The Sceptics have their Say

As the person sees the results of his good actions, and the difference it is making in the lives of not only others but his too, he will at some point let go of the attachment to gain recognition and reward, and continue doing good from his heart and soul."

> *"Fate is nothing but the deeds committed*
> *in a prior state of existence."*
> – Ralph Waldo Emerson

There was pin drop silence in the audience as the Prime Minister spoke - in all honesty, read most of their minds. He paused for a while to see if there were any new questions that had come up apart from the ones he already intended to answer, from his own list. He continued, "People have also criticised the government. Many think that this scheme has been initiated to get the minds of people, off the real issues plaguing the country. Well, we are tackling all the real issues the country is facing today. The root cause of all our troubles is that we have unfortunately been divided by hate. This grand idea will help us reunite once again, with love."

"Are you aware, my dear brothers and sisters, that just about five three hundred years ago, India was a land flowing with milk and honey? That Indian GDP constituted over 25% of the GDP of the entire world? Which means, over one fourth of all goods and services produced in the world over five centuries ago came from the Indian soil? At that time, the precious ingredient we had was unity, goodwill, and genuine concern for the welfare of one another."

"I would further like to clarify that we are not really interfering with karma here. Do you not reward your children when they have been good, when they have shown kindness and concern towards others? For the government, all of you are family. If a reward can be offered as a motivator and an incentive to ensure the less unfortunate are helped by those who can, we shall do so in every way possible."

"So, my beloved people of the nation, I hope I have answered some valid concerns that a few of you had brought up. It is always good to move on with a project of this scale with everybody on board. To conclude, I would like to repeat the words of our Father, Mahatma Gandhi - *First they ignore you, then they laugh at you, then they fight you, then you win.*"

"**Did** not the sceptics treat the Mahatma with laughter and disdain when he preached the path of resistance through non-violence? Did they not say freedom could never be won in this goody-goody manner? Did he not prove them all to be wrong when he won freedom for India, with the power of love? In fact, even Martin Luther King Jr was a huge admirer of the Mahatma's philosophy and approach. Let us doubt no more, and channelize all our efforts and energies into helping one another instead. In doing so, we will help ourselves. Everybody shall win in this way."

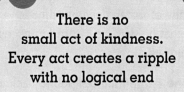

There is no
small act of kindness.
Every act creates a ripple
with no logical end

- Scott Adams

A Nobel Prize for a Noble Man

The inception of the Happyness Bank in India certainly brought about economic prosperity and raised the standard of living of its people. It was even more commendable since this was achieved through the route of harmony and co-operation, and by instilling the spirit of oneness amongst people. The habit of being and doing good was primarily the reason for the economic elevation which followed as a natural synergistic by-product.

Prime Minister Narottam Mehta was filled with pride, when leaders around the world began congratulating him, for lifting India up to the ranks of other developed nations. Yet, being the humble and honest leader that he was, he refused to accept the honour and take all the credit all by himself.

The Prime Minister publicly acknowledged the fact that the idea had come to him from Rohinton Talati, who had implemented it in an extremely detailed and effective manner, throughout his organisation. Rohinton was also not someone to hog the limelight for an idea that had actually originated elsewhere. He nobly nudged the media in Atul's direction, and give him credit for the sweeping positive changes that India, and now a few of her neighbouring countries were witnessing.

> A leader is best when people barely know he exists, when his work is done, his aim fulfilled, they will say: we did it ourselves
>
> – Lao Tzu

A Nobel Prize is the ultimate recognition of achievement, and one of the world's most prestigious honours. It is bestowed on those who have excelled and benefited the world in the fields of Physics, Chemistry, Physiology or Medicine, Literature, Peace and Economics. An annual and a very private affair, the Nobel Prize is conferred by a Norwegian Nobel Committee. Over 800 individuals and 21 organisations have been awarded till now, out of which 11 recipients have been Indians. Some of them include - include Rabindranath Tagore for Literature; Mother Teresa and Kailash Sathyarthi for Peace; and Amartya Sen for Economics.

The Nobel Prize is presented by the Chairman of the Norwegian Nobel Committee, in the presence of Their Majesties the King and Queen of Norway, the Government, Storting (The Norwegian Parliament), other representatives and an invited audience.

According to Alfred Nobel's will, the Peace Prize is to go to - *'whoever shall have done the most or the best work for fraternity between nations, for the abolition or reduction of standing armies and for the holding and promotion of peace congresses'*. The prize includes a medal, a personal diploma, and a large sum of prize money. The Nobel Prize award ceremony takes place in the Oslo City Hall, on December 10th each year - the date on which Alfred Nobel died. After the award ceremony, the Norwegian Nobel Committee hosts a banquet in honor of the Laureates.

Prime Minister Narottam Mehta as the Head of State, had nominated Atul for the Nobel Peace Prize - an honor which was richly and rightly deserved. With the world media focusing on Atul and his idea for a while, and seeing the proof of his achievements, it was only obvious that the Norwegian Nobel Committee chose Atul the winner of the Prize. Atul now joined the ranks of some of the greatest people in human history - Yasser Arafat, Nelson Mandela, Martin Luther King Jr., President Jimmy Carter of the USA, Mikhail Gorbachev, the Dalai Lama, and the likes. As much as Atul was over the moon on hearing this from the Prime Minister, he was equally stunned by the honour. By the time Atul could digest the news, he found himself on a special flight to Oslo, in Norway.

Atul was beyond flabbergasted by the sudden turn of events in his life. As his name was announced, and was asked to come on stage and receive the award, he felt a million butterflies flutter in his stomach. "Is this for real, or am I hallucinating once again?" Atul thought, as he pinched himself in literal sense while walking towards the stage. When the microphone was handed over to Atul, he froze and went blank, forgetting the content of his prepared acceptance speech. He had a similar feeling before addressing the townspeople of Gauraj Nagar, a couple of years ago. Back then, he had spontaneously promised them a solution to their depression, in order to get over the devastation, the town had been through, post the earthquake. This was a completely different ball game.

A Nobel Prize for a Noble Man

Gripping the microphone with trembling and sweating hands, Atul decided to do what he had always done. Close his eyes, say a short prayer, and surrender the outcome of what he would say to the Divine. There were goose-bumps on his skin, as he felt inspiration flow through his veins, and stars lit in his eyes. With a grip of iron, he held the microphone close to his chin, and with a voice of steel he thus began, "My humble greetings to Your Royal Highness, Your Royal Majesty, Honorable Chairman of the Norwegian Nobel Committee, Respected Members of the Storting and the Government, and all the other respected dignitaries gathered here today."

Happyness Bank

"**As** much as I receive this honour with deep humility and gratitude, I would be failing in my duty if I were not to mention the people to whom this Prize truly belongs. One, to all the seven billion human beings on this planet, who when united together as one, have the power to create miracles beyond imagination. Two, the Prime Minister and the people of my great country, India, who thought I was eligible enough to win such a prestigious award. Three, one of the world's greatest industrialists and a dear friend, Rohinton Talati, who had faith in my idea, when it was a small sapling. He invested time, money and energy in our town, which not only changed our lives, but has eventually changed the lives of millions of people worldwide."

A Nobel Prize for a Noble Man

"**Four,** the people of my town Gauraj Nagar, back in India. Without their initial patience, faith and trust in me and my words, this idea would never have taken off the ground. Five, my late wife and children, who I am sure are happily watching this right now, from somewhere in the universe. Last but not the least, the dearest of all, my late grandmother. She taught me the simplest truths and philosophies of the world, the most important of them being, the value of giving and sharing."

"**My** town Gauraj Nagar was warped in depression a few years ago, due to the devastating earthquake that it experienced. We lost everything - families, friends, personal belongings, homes and more than anything, our will to live. We battled our emotions for days together out of sheer frustration as to why God had played such a cruel joke on us. We sobbed tears of blood to say the least, including myself, looking for light at the end of the dark and doomed tunnel we felt we were living in."

"**The** Happyness Bank, or the **BANK** of **GOOD KARMA** then, was initiated for a simple reason - to motivate and assist people, to rise above the grotesque situation that they found themselves in. At that point I did not see anyone as being different from me. I felt everyone's pain in the depths of my heart when tragedy struck, and I also felt the relief and joy later when Gauraj Nagar went through a drastic change. This made me realise my dear brothers and sisters, that we are ONE. The world is ONE. We may well be divided by geographical lines, but at the core of our beings, we are united and bind together as a single entity.

Atul continued, "Human beings for quite some time now, have been deviating from their destined spiritual path to a ruthlessly materialistic one, at break neck speed. This I believe, needs to be reversed at the earliest. In this situation, governments and organisations can be rapid agents of change, as they control humongous resources. Most of them need to be gently reminded once again, that giving is as important as receiving, or growth, as most would understand it. Our Prime Minsiter and Rohinton Talati have amply proven this time and again, over the past few years."

"**Mankind** today is travelling at the speed of light towards self-destruction. Even though we are made of love, we have unfortunately been brought up in an environment of hate. We are constantly encouraged to

COMPETE with each other, rather than to CO-OPERATE. I know from experience that life's challenges can knock down the best of us - rich or poor. Our faith, patience and resilience gets tested time and again, and it may continue as well. We have only two choices - either sit where we are, sob our souls out and eventually die, or, get up, change ourselves and our perspectives, help others do the same, and leave this planet at our destined time, in peace and happiness. Not making a choice to do either is also in itself a choice. We just don't realise it."

"I truly believe that we are here, not only to evolve individually, but also help and guide others do the same. This is something every single religion and philosophy on earth has preached, for thousands of years. We forget that we are not just the body. We have within us the intangible energy of the mind and the soul. We take care of our bodies by eating well and exercising regularly. Some of us even take care of the mind with different kinds of **meditations and relaxation** techniques. Our often neglected soul needs to be fed with unconditional love that eventually propels us to do selfless acts of goodness. We gain instant calmness and composure from within once we understand this, which in simple words, gives us an experience of **TRUE HAPPINESS and BLISS.**

"Einstein's formula - $E = MC2$, was the idea that was touted as the idea of the 20th century. Unfortunately, people misused it to create the atom bomb, which went on to give more power to hatred. This was demonstrated to the world when it was dropped on the cities of Hiroshima and Nagasaki in 1945. We need a new idea now in the 21st century. An idea which propagates and encourages love instead of hate. Also, please do remember that every society is judged on how it treats the least fortunate amongst them."

"I have seen the results of growing with love with the Happyness Bank. This is an idea which I truly believe is capable of changing the world. Thank you, dear sisters and brothers. Have a wonderful evening. Lots of love and light, and God bless **you** all."

Atul left the stage to a resounding applause and some tears, thereby engraving the power of love and giving in the hearts of all billions around the world.

A Nobel Prize for a Noble Man

> "I tell you one thing- if you want peace, do not find fault with others. Rather, see your own faults. Learn to make the world your own. No one is a stranger my child; the whole world is your own."
> – Sri Sarada Devi

Appendix 1

List 1

Activity and Reward list for the Employees of Talati Industries.

Activity	Reward Points
Skill training - Provide six months of skill training to the currently unskilled/semi-skilled people of the locality.	5 Points for each person successfully trained.
Donation to Hospital - Donation of 2% of salary to hospital.	5 Points.
Donation to town public school - Donation of 2% of salary to school.	5 Points.
Sponsoring the education of a girl child from the locality.	5 Points for each Girl Child sponsored.
Contribution from the wives of the employees - 120 hours of social work in one year which could include teaching, skill-sharing, etc.	5 Points.
Contribution from the children of the employees - Donation of their old clothes/books/computers/etc. 1 point for every Rs. 5000/- worth of items.	Maximum 5 Points.

Points	Rewards
25	1- month salary as bonus
50	2 months' salary as bonus
75	4 months' salary as bonus

List 2

Activity and Reward List for people outside the organisation

Activity	Reward Points
Successfully undergoing training in any skill-set which would be required by the factory.	10 Points on successful completion of each skill training.
Allowing one's wife to work in the factory.	5 Points.
Sending all the children in the family to school.	5 Points.
Having a bathroom within the house.	5 Points.
Keeping one's own house and surrounding area clean.	5 Points.
Preparing food once a week for his trainer/immediate boss/sponsor.	5 Points per week.

Points	Rewards
25	Free Life Insurance Policy.
50	Free Medical Policy and substantial discount in purchasing any product of Talati Industries.
75	A permanent job in the factory, with joining bonus.

Appendix 2

CATEGORY INDEX

Activities will be given points ranging from 1 - 5 points depending on the intrinsic nature, level of difficulty and the possible frequency of that activity. *To insure equality, every member can accumulate maximum 5 points per category per year.*

Periodically, *Happyness Bank* (HB) will add, update and circulate, list of activities.

Category no	Particulars
1	Activities related to teaching
2	Activities related to donation of Money
3	Activities related to donation of Body organs/parts.
4	Spiritual and Religious activities
5	Activities related to cleaning/improving environment.
6	Volunteering for relief work after natural disaster / calamities.
7	Volunteering to offer Professional help free of cost.
8	Volunteering to work in local NGO's / International Organisations with which Happiness Bank has a tie up.
9	Heroic activities. Acts of bravery done in good faith to help/save someone.
10	Volunteer work for HB(Happiness Bank).
11	Sponsoring education/skill training of employees / children of employees, who directly work for you.
12	Winning national / international awards in any field recognised by Happiness Bank.
13	Voting for local bodies/state legislature / parliament.
14	Filing income tax returns in time
15	Activities related to skill training.
16	Inspiring 25 or more people to open their Happiness Bank account.

Category 1 - Activities related to teaching

Under this category there will be two kinds of activities.

The first kind of activity will entail teaching in schools/colleges/ formal educational institutes for 'X' number of hours on a topic of his/her expertise.

Second kind of activity will entail conducting 1- 2 day seminars / workshops on topics of his/her expertise.

Needless to say, HB will periodically publish a list of School/colleges having such teaching requirement.

No.	Description	Points	Remarks
1.1	Free 1 - 2 Day long seminars with HB authorised institutes by people who have expertise in a particular subject. E.g finance, leadership, yoga, soft skills, etc.	1 point per seminar	
1.2	Free teaching of a subject in a school/college. This could be like teaching something 1 hour a day for 2 times a week. Maybe 1 or 2 Subjects for a semester. It is envisaged that such teaching could be of 20-30 hours in a semester.	1 point for every 5 hours for teaching.	

Category 2 - Activities related to donation of money

Under this category, other than plain cash donation, different options will be given to people, so that they can donate money for a cause which is close to their heart. For contributions in activities other than cash donation, HB will have an internal assessment system to decide the points depending on the unique nature of that activity.

No.	Description	Points	Remarks
2.1	Cash donation.	1 point for every Rs.10,000/-	Maximum 2 points for this sub-category so as to prevent advantage to the rich due to income inequality.
2.2	Sponsoring a Child's education	1 point	Periodically, HB will publish a list of children requiring sponsorship for their yearly education.
2.3	Donation in kind. E.g. Clothes/ books, etc over a certain value	2 points max	HB will formulate a mechanism / system to access, the value of such goods and accordingly gift points.
2.4	Sponsoring meals for the poor.	1 point	The money donated in this sub - category will be used specifically for sponsoring meals for the poor.
2.5	Adopting the yearly expenses of girl Child.	2 points	Under this sub - category, donations of money and monies worth will be used to meet the yearly expenses of a girl child.

178

Category 3 - Activities related to donation of blood and body organs/parts.

Under this category there are two scenarios

Scenario 1) Signing up to donate a body part after death.
E.g. Signing up to donate eyes after death.

Scenario 2) Donating body parts/fluids when alive.
E.g. Donating kidney, blood, etc.

No.	Description	Points	Remarks
3.1	Blood Donation. 2 times a year.	1 point per donation	Maximum 2 points per year.
3.2	Signing up for eye donation / donation of any other organ after death.	5 points	Points will accrue in the year when a person signs up for donation.
3.3	Donating your kidney, organ, while you are alive.	5 points	Points will accrue in the year when a person signs up for donation.

Category 4 - Spiritual and Religious activities

Under this category a person will earn points for indulging in spiritual and religious activities. Since there are many religions and each religion has its own unique spiritual and religious activity, it will be the endeavor of *Happyness Bank* to include as many activities as possible based on the recommendations of religious leaders to give maximum opportunity to people following different religion to indulge in such activities and earn points.

The list given below is only illustrative and not exhaustive and its aim is to give an idea of how different points can be awarded for different activities depending on the nature and the difficulty to perform that activity.

No.	Description	Points	Remarks
4.1	Writing Mantras E.g. Om Namah Shivay	1 point for every Rs.10,000	Maximum 2 points per year
4.2	Visiting spiritual places as recognised by *Happyness Bank.* E.g. For Hindus - Vaishnodevi, Tirupati, Amarnath Yatra For Muslims - Mecca, Madina	2 points per place	Maximum 2 points per year
4.3	Attending church / temple / mosque for more than twenty - six times a year.	2 points	Maximum 2 points per year
4.4	Participating in religious ceremony as per the weekly / monthly list circulated out by the *Happiness Bank.*	1 point per participation	From time to time the working committee of *Happiness Bank* will circulate lists which will give details of the date, time and venue of religious ceremonies.

Category 5 - Activities related to cleaning / improving environment

Under this category members of HB will be given points for participating in activities related to the cleaning and the improving of environment.

No.	Description	Points	Remarks
1	Sapling Plantation	1	1 point for every participation.
2	Cleaning of beaches	1	1 point for every participation.
3	Cleaning of roads	1	1 point for every participation.
4	Participation in a peace walk for a particular issue.	1	1 point for every participation.
5	Active participant in a forum promoting any public / social issue. E.g. Aids awareness, Dowry Prohibition, etc.	1	1 point for every participation.

Category 6 - Volunteering for relief work after natural disaster/ calamities

Under this category members of HB will be given points for participating in activities related to the cleaning and the improving of environment.

No.	Description	Points	Remarks
6.1	Volunteering for relief work after natural disaster / calamities.	1 - 5	HB will formulate various schemes for disaster relief and points will be given on the nature and difficulty of the task to be performed.

Category 7 - Volunteering to offer Professional help free of cost

Under this category, members can accumulate points by offering their professional expertise free of costs. Doctors, Lawyers, Chartered Accountants and any other member having proficiency in any particular field can offer their services..

No.	Description	Points	Remarks
7.1	Volunteering to offer professional help free of cost.	1 - 5	As per schemes formulated by HB.

Category 8 - Volunteering to work in local NGOs / International Organisations, which will have a tie up with the Happyness Bank

Happyness Bank will be tying up with thousands of well-known / credible NGO's and organisations who work for the betterment of the needy. Periodically, a list of such organisations will be published/circulated. Points will be given on the number of hours a person invests in working for different causes taken up by different organisations.

No.	Description	Points	Remarks
8.1	Working 20 hours with 'ABC' Organisation helping mentally challenged children.	1 for every 10 hours invested.	

Category 9 - Heroic activities. Acts of bravery done in good faith to help / save someone.

Under this category, a person that puts on a brave act in good faith to help someone, or to save someone in distress shall earn points. Example: A person saves another from drowning. A person takes a bleeding accident victim to hospital. A person saves a girl from being molested, etc. This category will also recognise people who have won bravery awards.

No.	Description	Points	Remarks
9.1	Heroic activities. Acts of bravery done in good faith to help / save someone.	5	The authenticity of such an act shall be verified through eye witnesses, media report, hospital records, etc.
9.2	Winning a bravery award from a recognised organisation / government.		

Category 10 - Volunteering to work for HB (Happyness Bank)

Happyness Bank, itself will need several thousands of people to work for it. People volunteering to work will be given points as per time invested and nature of work. Also contributions in the form of ideas, and in the form ofsuggestions of new categories/sub categories to be added to the various categories will be rewarded with points.

No.	Description	Points	Remarks
10.1	Volunteering to work as per assigned task.	1 point for every 10 hours of work.	
10.2	Suggesting ideas which are accepted and implemented by HB.	5 points.	

Category 11 - Sponsoring the education / skill training of employees / children of employees, who directly work for you.

Under this category, members of the Happyness Bank will be encouraged to help or assist people working for them. E.g. drivers, house help, car cleaner, laundry men, watchmen, etc. Sponsoring the education or skill training of these employees / children of employees, in recognised public school / other credible teaching organisations, will help earn the members their points.

No.	Description	Points	Remarks
11.1	Sponsoring the education / skill training of employees / children of employees, who directly work for you.	1 - 5	Depending on the extent of help and the schemes formulated by the managing committee of HB, members will be able to earn 1- 5 points.

Category 12 - Winning national / international awards in any field recognised by Happyness Bank.

There are several types / kinds of award given by Internationals Organisations / Government / Credible private Organisations. Happyness Bank shall recognise and make a exhaustive list of such awards, and the list shall be updated with members recommendations.

Example: International awards - Nobel Peace Prize, Magsaysay, etc
National awards - Padmabhushan, Padmashree, etc
Awards by private bodies - Zee Films Awards, Times of India Award, etc
Any person winning an award recognised by Happyness Bank can earn points.

No.	Description	Points	Remarks
12.1	Winning national / international awards in any field recognised by Happiness Bank.	5	Maximum 5 points in a year. Thus, even if someone wins 2 awards, he will still get 5 points.

Category 13 - Voting for local bodies / state legislature / parliament.

There are basically three occasions to vote.

Occasion 1) Local Bodies, **Occasion 2)** State Legislature, **Occasion 3)** Parliament at the Center.

No.	Description	Points	Remarks
13.1	Voting for local bodies / state legislature / parliament	5 per vote	It may happen that in a particular year, there is no requirement for voting and therefore, no points will be earned. It may also happen that in some years there may be an occasion to vote 2 times. In such a situation, maximum 5 points can only be earned for that year.

Category 14 - Filling income tax returns in time

Under this category a person who files his tax return in time i.e. 30th
July or any other dated as announced by the Government will earn points.

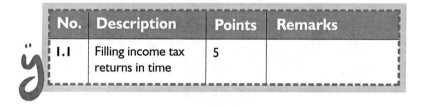

No.	Description	Points	Remarks
1.1	Filling income tax returns in time	5	

Category 15 - Activites related to skill training

Under this category members having any kind of skill can accumulate
points by teaching their skill to needy unskilled people for free of cos.

E.g. Electricians, plumbers, cooks, tailors, etc. will be able to earn
points by teaching their skills to unskilled people.

No.	Description	Points	Remarks
15.1	Volunteering for imparting free skill training to the unskilled and unprivileged.	1 - 5	Points will be given on the number of people successfully taught.

Appendix 2

Category 16 - Inspiring 25 or more people to open their Happyness Bank account.

Under this Category any Happyness Bank Account holder can earn points by inspiring 25 or more people to open their Happyness Bank Account.

No.	Description	Points	Remarks
16.1	Inspiring 25 or more people to open their Happiness Bank account.	5	

Epilogue

Happÿness Bank

> " Thirty Years Later "

In the last five thousand years of written history, books have been replete with wars and violence. Every century has been deadlier than the previous one. Mankind made a lot of progress, but, unfortunately at the great cost of war and violence. We managed to reach Mars, connect with people through television, radio, and internet, but failed to re connect with our own inner selves. We unfortunately chose to ignore and forget the fact that if given an opportunity, man has infinite potential to do good.

By 2047, the Happyness Bank scheme had changed the lives of billions of people around the world, since almost a hundred countries chose to adopt the scheme into their system. The United Nations also actively supported the idea, and formed a separate committee that would assist countries in the implementation and execution of the Happyness Bank.

Children who were just five years old when they were given their first **HAPPYNESS PASSBOOKS**, were now thirty-five. There was a stark difference in the behaviour and thought process of this new generation, and the previous one.

Due to this behavioral change spanning thirty years, these young souls had a completely different perspective about life and its challenges, together with also having a different vision of the future of mankind, and planet earth. Young entrepreneurs were innovating and competing as before, but there was a huge difference in their approach towards business and commerce. They now had more intentions to give and help, rather than just take and exploit.

The earth had become better place to live in, as the death spin of mankind towards self-destruction had been reversed. The simple yet effective idea of the **3 R's - RECOGNIZING, RECORDING** and **REWARDING** good work, with a simple passbook, had brought about unfathomable amounts of positivity in people.

Global terrorism and other criminal activities were at their lowest, resulting in an obvious increase in the **HAPPYNESS INDEX**. The last three decades had been the first decades where progress was made by co - operation, love and goodness, instead of annexations, war and destruction.

Through the *Happyness Bank,* mankind had at last discovered a way to harness its most potent energy - the energy of **LOVE** and **GOODNESS**, and had achieved its most cherished goal - the goal to be **HAPPY**.

About the Authors

Vishal Gupta

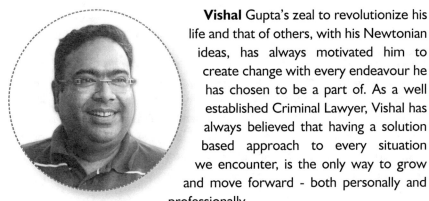

Vishal Gupta's zeal to revolutionize his life and that of others, with his Newtonian ideas, has always motivated him to create change with every endeavour he has chosen to be a part of. As a well established Criminal Lawyer, Vishal has always believed that having a solution based approach to every situation we encounter, is the only way to grow and move forward - both personally and professionally.

Having passed out from the prestigious Cathedral and John Connon school Vishal went on to pursue Computer Enginnering from Pune University . The entrepreneural bug caught up with him at an early age of 26. He founded NICE (National Institute of Computer Education), imparting "Parallel Education"- a revolutionary mode of computer education which complemented regular school studies, to children between the ages of three to ten.. Vishal's foray into Internet and software Consultancy was also a parallel phenomena. Soon after, With his helicopter vision, Vishal founded and formally launched in India, Aryabhatt Linux- the first Indian distribution of the of the Linux operating system (OS), in May 2000.

Vishal has always been a multifaceted thought leader and brand strategist with his vast experiences in various corporate sectors, heading teams and companies. Being extremely enthusiastic about writing, Vishal is known to sleep with a pen around his neck, just incase he receives yet another revolutionising idea. His passion for writing and education led him to regularly write a column for over two years in a well-known publication called Express Computers. A lover of all forms of art, Vishal continuously works on honing his creativity skills, bringing them to life by applying them in every project he initiates. He is a well-trained photographer and a multi-linguist.

Vishal's sensitivity towards injustice in various areas of the world and life motivated him to find a formal and systemised way to assist humanity. This urge led him to add another feather in his hat of knowledge and experience, that of Criminal Law. His humility and passion for learning helped him officially study and complete his degree in law, even though he was a highly successful and accomplished business man by then, heading and leading various companies.

Spiritually inclined from a very young age and with certain life experiences along his path, Vishal learnt the immense powers of Gratitude & Giving, which played a large role in making him write Happyness Bank. Having immense faith in the goodness of love, life and people in general, Vishal truly lives and acts with the conviction that 'Service to Mankind, is Service to God.'

About the Authors

Cyrus Gonda

Cyrus is a qualified MENSA international life-member and a rank - holding MBA from NMIMS, MUMBAI University.

Cyrus is the author / co - author of many best - selling management books on the subjects of leadership, selling excellence, customer experience excellence and soft skills; which are used by leading corporate houses to profitably train their staff in these areas. He possesses rich and varied experience with leading MNCs in the manufacturing and service sectors, in operations as well as administrative roles, both in India and overseas. Cyrus currently is the head of department - Strategic communication, at Rizvi management institutes, Mumbai and also the Jt. Managing Director of the cutting - edge leadership and management consultancy firm - Brains Trust India.

He is a communicator and logician par excellence; a spontaneous, entertaining and enlightening speaker. His training workshops are filled with interesting business anecdotes, of which he has a memorable wealth at his disposal for every occasion.

Authors' Note

The fundamental philosophy behind the concept outlined in this book, is based on 3 R's - **RECOGNIZING, RECORDING** and **REWARDING** good work. This process is carried out with the allotment and use of a Passbook, and the accompanying **TWO LISTS.** List 1 defines the good deeds, and List 2 enumerates the places where the good deeds laid out in List 1 can be performed.

Who all can benefit with the implementation of the Happyness Bank **scheme?**

1) **Families**: Parents can give their children the **HAPPYNESS PASSBOOK. List 1** and **List 2** can be filled up as per the personal choices and needs of parents. A child that grows up to become a good human being is as important as being a good student academically.

2) **Schools & Colleges**: The role of academic institutions is not only to provide theoretical knowledge, but also to develop the character of its students. The authors highly recommend that every school and college should give their students a **HAPPYNESS PASSBOOK,** along with the **TWO LISTS.** Performing and recording all their good deeds will not only benefit and motivate the child, but also benefit the society as a whole. Children are balls of love and innocence. If we can harness and maintain their goodness by motivating them from an early age, there is no question that our future citizens will be of a higher calibre, and more compassionate towards each other.

3) **Corporates**: Even though corporate houses are already doing good work in the field of Corporate Social Responsibility, the authors suggest a change in the method of doing so. We recommend that every employee be given a **HAPPYNESS PASSBOOK** with the accompanying **TWO LISTS,** which include good deeds according to each organization's corporate values. The good work done by each employee should be recorded over the course of tenure with an organization.

4) **World - renowned, higher - education institutions**: If reputed institutes of higher learning such as the IITs and the IIMs incorporate as part of their admission criteria, the Happyness Bank Passbook,they would be belting out not only hundreds of thousands whiz kids, but also good, loving and compassionate human beings.

5) **Governments**: Presently, even after spending billions of dollars, governments are unable to reach out to its citizens effectively. In all honesty, with the current mess that the world is in, it is impossible for any single government to reach out successfullyto all of its people. Therefore, the best policy is to create conditions and environments that encourage citizens to help one another. The Happyness Bank scheme is capable of solving nearly all the problems which afflict a nation. It has the potential to increase literacy and employment, and decrease crime and poverty. It can motivate people to be more loving and tolerant citizens, who would be willing to work with co - operation, rather than cutting each other's throats in competition.

If any individual wishes to avail our assistance to incorporate the Happyness Bank scheme in their institute/organization, in a customized and structured manner, we would be more than happy to help.

The authors could be contacted on:

Website: happyness-bank.com
Email: happynessbank@gmail.com | contact@happyness-bank.com
Mobile No.: 9820308218

Happyness Bank

"IF YOU KNEW WHAT I KNOW ABOUT THE POWER OF GIVING, YOU WOULD NOT LET A SINGLE MEAL PASS WITHOUT SHARING IT IN SOME WAY."

- BUDDHA